ON
MAX
WEBER

KARL JASPERS
ON
MAX
WEBER

Edited with Introduction and Notes

JOHN DREIJMANIS

Translated from the German by Robert J. Whelan

Paragon House

NEW YORK

First edition, 1989
Published in the United States by
Paragon House Publishers
90 Fifth Avenue
New York, NY 10011

Max Weber: A Commemorative Address (1920),
Max Weber: Politician, Scientist, Philosopher
(1932), and *Observations on Max Weber's Political*
Thought are excerpted from Karl Jaspers, *Aneignung*
und Jaspers. Briefwechsel 1926-1969 (Munich: R.
Piper and Company Verlag, 1985). *Max Weber:*
Concluding Characterization (1960–1961) is
excerpted from Die groBen Philosophen NachlaB
(Munich: R. Piper and Company Verlag, 1981).
Letters to Hannah Arendt are excerpted from
Hannah Arendt/Karl Jaspers Briefwechsel.
1926–1969 (Munich: R. Piper and Company
Verlag, 1985). All the above reprinted by
arrangement with Hans Saner.

TRANSLATION LINE EDITED BY
PETER KEIL AND THOMAS E.
McCARTHY OF THE COLLEGE OF
STATEN ISLAND, THE CITY
UNIVERSITY OF NEW YORK.

Library of Congress Cataloging-in-Publication Data

Jaspers, Karl, 1883–1969.
On Max Weber.

Includes bibliographical references and index.
 1. Weber, Max, 1864–1920—Contributions in
political
science. 2. Germany—Intellectual life. I. Dreijmanis,
John. II. Title.

Contents

Translator's Note

This translation of Karl Jaspers's essays is as literal as possible within the limits of good English. In those few cases in which a literal translation is unintelligible, a liberal one was rendered without deviation from the author's intent and the context. The word *"Scheitern"* has been rendered as "floundering" to indicate Jaspers's more precise meaning.

At its best, a translation purports to reproduce the ideas and events of the original—not all can be, however, but enough so that we regret our ignorance of the original, realizing the effectiveness of the author's voice in his native tongue.

The translator wishes to thank the editor for checking the typescript and reading the proofs.

R.J.W.
University of Lowell

Preface

S ince the introduction deals with Karl Jaspers's writings on Max Weber and their relationship, it is unnecessary to dwell upon these matters here. A few words need to be said, however, about the German texts used for the translation. The 1920, 1932, and 1962 essays are from Jaspers's *Aneignung und Polemik. Gesammelten Reden und Aufsätze zur Geschichte der Philosophie,* edited by Hans Saner (Munich: R. Piper & Co. Verlag, 1968), pages 409–96. Except for the titles of the 1920 and 1932 works they are identical to the originals. The first and second editions of the 1920 memorial address in 1921 and 1926 had the title: *Max Weber. Rede bei der von der Heidelberger Studentenschaft am 17. Juli 1920 veranstalteten Trauerfeier* [Tübingen: J.C.B. Mohr (Paul Siebeck), 1921].

The 1932 essay was originally entitled *Max Weber. Deutsches Wesen im politischen Denken, im*

Forschen und Philosophieren (Oldenburg: Gerhard Stalling, 1932), changed in 1946 and subsequent editions to *Max Weber. Politiker, Forscher, Philosoph* (Bremen: Johannes Storm Verlag, 1946). It contained a footnoted reference to Weber's works—mainly the political works. Because these are now widely known and available, the footnote has been deleted. There are few other footnotes, and for this reason the essays have been, wherever possible, annotated. The 1932 essay appeared in Jaspers's *Three Essays: Leonardo, Descartes, Max Weber,* translated by Ralph Mannheim (New York: Harcourt, Brace & World, 1964), pages 187–274, but it was a loose translation with many omissions. The quotations from Weber have been checked against the originals wherever possible. The piece entitled *Max Weber: Concluding Characterization* is taken from Jaspers's *Die großen Philosophen Nachlaß,* edited by Hans Saner (Munich: R. Piper & Co. Verlag, 1981), Volume 1, pages 641–651, much of it dating from 1960–61. Finally, the two letters are from *Hannah Arendt/ Karl Jaspers. Briefwechsel 1926–1969,* edited by Lotte Köhler and Hans Saner (Munich: R. Piper & Co. Verlag, 1985), pages 671–73, 695–96. The editor gratefully acknowledges Hans Saner's permission to use previously published material.

A number of people were helpful in this undertaking. I am grateful to Eduard Baumgarten; Edward

Shils, University of Chicago; Nicolaus Sombart, Free University of Berlin; Ilse Dronberger, University of Mainz; Martin Green, Tufts University; Robert J. Whelan, University of Lowell; Johannes Winckelman, Director of the Max Weber Institute, University of Munich; Martin Riesebrodt and Karl-Ludwig Ay of the Commission for Social and Economic History, Bavarian Academy of the Sciences; and Luna Carne-Ross. Finally, it is to Hans Saner that I owe the greatest debt. This book would have been impossible without his generous cooperation.

JOHN DREIJMANIS

Introduction

K arl Jaspers was born in Oldenburg near the North Sea on 23 February 1883 and died in Basel on 26 February 1969. He first studied law at Heidelberg and Munich, but soon turned in disappointment to philosophy and finally to medicine at Berlin, Göttingen, and finally at Heidelberg, where he secured his M.D. degree in 1909. In 1910 he married a Jewish woman, Gertrud Mayer.

Jaspers had, however, a secret desire to pursue an academic career in psychiatry or psychology. In 1913, aided by a recommendation from Max Weber (1864–1920), he became a lecturer in psychology at Heidelberg and published a text on psychopathology,[1] which was well-received.

Despite Jaspers's earlier rejection of philosophy due to its betrayal by philosophy professors, he decided to make it his life's work. This decision coincided with his appointment in 1921 as professor of philosophy at Heidelberg, a post he accepted after declining offers from Greifswald and Kiel. Jaspers wanted to remain in Heidelberg, "that unique town, intellectually so spirited, and through memories so dear."[2] By his own admission, he was not ready for such a demanding task, but the challenge was great: ". . . when the intellectual world is empty of philosophy, it becomes the task at least to bear witness to philosophy, to direct the attention to the great philosophers, to try to stop confusion, and to encourage in our youth the interest in real philosophy."[3]

Jaspers remained at Heidelberg until his dismissal by the National Socialists in 1937, reinstated in 1945 by the American occupation authorities. In 1948 he accepted an offer from Basel, teaching there until his retirement in 1961. Jaspers had concluded that Heidelberg was no longer his home. Disappointed by the poor living conditions and by his colleagues' rejection of his work on the question of German guilt,[4] he feared the probability of remaining at Heidelberg as an interdicted academic.[5]

Jaspers met Weber for the first time in 1909. A close friendship soon developed between the emerging existentialist philosopher and the already well-known founder of modern sociology as a scientific discipline. Jaspers soon joined Max and Marianne Weber's inner circle of friends, which consisted of Friedrich Gundolf (1880–1931), literary historian at Heidelberg; and Georg von Lukács (1885–1971), the later famous Hungarian Marxist philosopher.

Apart from Kant, Kierkegaard, and Nietzsche, Weber was one of Jaspers' most important mentors. From very early in his life, Jaspers's "longing went towards greatness. I felt reverence for great philosophers, who are irrecoverable for all of us, from whom we get our standards and whom we yet do not deify."[6] He found such greatness in Weber. Jaspers and his wife discovered in him:

> . . . ever and again the road to an irreplaceable assurance. Thinking of him, even in dark hours, this was always still a guarantee. In him we could know what a man is capable of, what trustworthiness and depth of the spirit is, what German can be. The question, what would Max Weber say, became the claim to envisage the essential. The content of his being, once taken up in youth, became a lasting source, out of which throughout a lifetime, ever new things are capable of growing.[7]

The two men shared certain fundamental beliefs. Neither had a philosophical system because both believed man cannot comprehend the whole and the absolute due to the limitations and floundering of his knowledge. They felt that knowledge can be gained only of particular realities—not the total picture: knowledge is relative. Both rejected metaphysical concepts and Marxism. Jaspers saw in Weber one who pointed to the limitations of science in order to protect the existential freedom of the individual. Politics for both could exist only in freedom.

Jaspers came to regard Weber as the "greatest German of our era."[8] In 1966–67 he even saw him as "spiritually the greatest man of our time" and as the "Galilei of the *Geisteswissenschaften.*"[9] In all probability Jaspers regarded Weber as the prototype of the demonic personality in scholarship—"profound, decisive, a turning point in thinking and yet without a system, without successors, without a proper school. . . ."[10] Weber's death in 1920 was seen by him as an earthshaking event: ". . . it was for me as though the world had changed."[11] Ernst Moritz Manasse expressed it well when he wrote that Weber is the "spirit of Jaspers' philosophy."[12]

Despite Jaspers's great admiration for Weber, the relationship was not one of master and disciple. As Jaspers said to Gundolf, "to become a Weberian is impossible."[13] More fundamentally, Jaspers declared: "Discipleship is disastrous and cannot be carried through in truthfulness."[14] Jaspers criticized Weber as late as 1916 for wasting time on political matters of the day "instead of objectivising himself."[15] He also did not have as favorable an opinion of Prussia and Bismarck as Weber did. Yet, Weber remained the ideal statesman.

Weber's basic political views, however, Jaspers "simply learned and took over."[16] Until 1914 he was apolitical, but World War I and his association with Weber changed that. Through Weber, Jaspers also began to think in national terms. It took the advent of National Socialism for him to begin publishing his political thoughts. First came *Die geistige Situation der Zeit. Politisches Bewußtsein in unserer Zeit* (Berlin: Walter de Gruyter & Co., 1931), translated by Eden and Cedar Paul as *Man in the Modern Age* (London: G. Routledge & Sons, 1933), followed the next year by the second and the longest of Jaspers's works on Weber.

The Hitler period was for Jaspers a time of reflection. He saw that philosophy was not without political consequences. Jaspers and his wife considered emigration but dismissed the idea, even rejecting an offer from Paris. Heidelberg was still to him "spiritually the only home. . . ."[17] Jaspers was willing to go to Basel for some guest lectures in 1941, but Berlin authorities refused his wife permission to leave the country.

The collapse of the Weimar Republic, the rise and demise of the Third Reich, and the division of Germany and the Allied occupation led Jaspers to think more and more about politics in general and

German politics in particular. Echoing Weber's distinction between the "principle ethic" and the "responsibility ethic" Jaspers saw a tension in politics between integrity and success. A statesman is great when he does "what he is willing to stand by forever."[18] Like Weber, Jaspers preferred rule by great statesmen (Weber's charismatic leader): "the men of judgment and vision—a minority, to be sure, but one that would be aristocratic in the literal sense of the word. . . ."[19] A conversation in 1919 between Weber and General Erich Ludendorff (1865–1937), after Weber's return from Versailles as a member of the German delegation, illustrates Weber's and Jaspers's preference for plebiscitary leadership. Weber defined democracy as a system in which "the people elect a leader whom they trust. Then the elected says, 'Now shut your mouths and obey. The people and the parties are no longer permitted to contradict him.' "[20] To this Ludendorff replied: "Such a 'democracy' could appeal to me!"[21] Weber then added: "Afterwards the people can judge. If the leader has made mistakes—to the gallows with him! . . ."[22]

Jaspers had hoped that after World War II there would be a truly new beginning in German politics. The task was to establish a new and democratic state, but not even the Basic Law was submitted to a plebiscite. The Federal Republic of Germany lacked and still lacks a political ideal. There is "no sense where we come from or where we are going, and hardly a present concern other than with our private welfare, with the good life, and with security."[23] Jaspers saw danger in the possibility of the political party oligarchy leading to "an authoritarian state, and this in turn to dictatorship."[24] Although this was written in 1966 at the beginning of the CDU/CSU-SPD grand coalition, it was an unfounded fear.

Few major German philosophers have been so critical of German political institutions and behavior. In his last years Jaspers was as politically active as Weber had ever been, even giving radio and television lectures on German stations.[25]

Unlike Weber, however, Jaspers was preoccupied with the question, What is German? He regarded the political aspect as only one dimension, "an unhappy one at that, a history which proceeds from one catastrophe to another."[26] He concluded that what is genuinely German "lives in the great spiritual realm, spiritually creating and battling. . . ."[27] In June 1967 Jaspers ceased to be a political German; he became a Swiss citizen.

Jaspers's rejection of the German Federal Republic was preceded by considerable doubts about Weber. In 1963 he saw some letters that Weber had exchanged with Else Jaffé, nee von Richthofen (1874–1974), a former student.[28] Weber's wife, Marianne, had suspected a love affair, and after Weber's death asked Jaspers about the possibility. Jaspers dismissed the idea, declaring "Max Weber was the truth itself."[29] It was not until 5 May 1967, when Jaspers wrote to Jaffé, that he discovered Weber's infidelity to his wife. He had difficulty characterizing Weber: "I ask perhaps: What happens with a man to whom truth is above everything else?"[30] The more he read Weber's works, the more he saw "a titanic trouble in emptiness."[31] Jaspers's discovery caused him considerable distress. He would have revised his evaluation of Weber had he sufficient time for it.[32]

"Throughout my life I have confronted the task of trying to understand his [Weber's] reality,"[33] wrote Jaspers in 1957. Of the three people in Weber's inner circle, only Jaspers wrote at length about him. On 17 July 1920 he gave a commemorative address at the invitation of the Heidelberg student association. The university senate forbade an official ceremony. In 1932 Jaspers's thoughts once more turned to Weber. During the 1960–61 academic year he again gave some lectures on Weber. In 1962 Jaspers wrote a short piece on Weber's political thought for a *Festschrift* for Edgar Salin (1892–1974), a political economist at Heidelberg, Kiel, and Basel who knew both Weber and Jaspers.

The 1920 address broadly examined Weber's life and scholarly contributions. Jaspers saw Weber's work as "fragmentary," reminiscent of Weber's characterization of scientific works in general as "imperfect" and to be "surpassed."[34] In the last year of his life Jaspers described his own work to his friends as a "fragment,"[35] but in a more conventional sense of the word. Weber's scholarly interests were wide and unbounded. Science's goal was, for him, knowledge set free from value-oriented constraints. Yet, Weber approached his scientific endeavors with great intensity and passion. He had regarded *"passionate* devotion"[36] as an integral part of one's scientific vocation.

Weber was a patriot. He believed in Germany and was ready to enter politics if and when called, but not on his own initiative. It can be argued, however, that Weber wanted to be called to assume great political responsibility; when no call came he sought to enter politics on his own, but without much success. Jaspers saw correctly that Weber was neither merely a politician nor a scholar because, to him, neither politics nor scholarship held a central and absolute meaning. Believing Weber must be seen in totality, Jaspers concluded, somewhat surprisingly, that Weber was a philosopher.

In the 1932 work Jaspers elaborated upon the themes first raised in 1920, maintaining that Weber "was the richest and deepest realization of the meaning of floundering in our time."[37] It was, however, a true floundering of an individual's historical existence. Weber criticized the pseudo-constitutionalism under Wilhelm II (1888–1918, [1859–1941]) for not producing true statesmen and observed Germany's decline, powerless to change it. Weber was not called upon to enter politics; nor would the people have followed him had he become a political leader.

Jaspers attributed Weber's political failure to his lack of the shrewdness and unscrupulousness normally possessed by politicians. His ethics made him unwilling to lie, dissemble, or manipulate the people. While this was a contributing factor, Weber was aware of his own limitations and of the qualities needed in a politician. As he noted: "And in any case it is not the qualities that make him an excellent scholar and academic teacher which make him a leader in the domain of practical life or, more specifically, in politics."[38]

Weber's contributions to value analysis and his demonstration of a relationship between capitalism and the Protestant ethic have been well described by Jaspers. Missing from Jaspers's analysis is an adequate discussion of Weber's ideal type in social science and of his contributions to the study of public administration and political leadership, including charismatic authority. In fairness to Jaspers, however, it should be noted that he planned to write at some length on the latter, contrasting Weber and Adolf Hitler (1889–1945) as charismatic leaders.

Jaspers has perceptively evaluated Weber the man. He has quite rightly drawn attention to the contradictory traits in Weber: his passion for knowledge and scientific work, and his indifference towards his achievements and his belief that all knowledge is relative. There was in Weber a powerful quest for truth.

Jaspers's posthumously published writings mainly consist of short notes for his 1960–61 lectures. They contain some dramatic statements about their relationship. Jaspers emphatically regrets that Weber's greatness was not recognized and properly used.

The 1962 essay is somewhat of an anticlimax, dealing essentially with Weber's views on World War I and whether or not he would have given allegiance to any German state. In 1960 Jaspers became eligible for Swiss citizenship. His concern with Weber's possible allegiance to Germany under different political systems foreshadowed his own rejection of the German Federal Republic.

Jaspers has dealt with Weber in his totality, stressing the fragmentary nature of his work, his quest for truth, his concern with Germany's world position, and his lack of success in politics. Jaspers's later doubts about Weber stemmed from his great disappointment that Weber had not lived up to his somewhat idealized portrait of him. Weber had been, to use a phrase by Nietzsche, "human, all too human" in his infidelity to Marianne. Jaspers's criticism of Weber on these grounds has not substantially diminished Weber's importance, but has rather made him more human.

Max Weber:
A Commemorative Address

(1920)

———————————

To say a word upon the death of Max Weber is really an empty gesture. A great man is honored when each one in his small way adopts his works and attempts to work with his ideas in order to realize what he made possible. That can only happen over an extended period of time, but we ought now to talk about it in the abstract, cognizant of what we had and what we lost.

Max Weber appeared to many of us as a *philosopher*. It is not appropriate that this great man be claimed by a particular profession or science. If he was a philosopher, then perhaps he was the only one in our time and in a different sense than someone might be today. His philosophical existence is more than we are able to comprehend at the moment. We must first learn its meaning, first acquire it for ourselves. I will make an inadequate attempt to speak of it. I am not speaking, however, about the unique human being whom we loved.

If we look at his work, as we see it here before us, we find an abundance of individual works. But all are really *fragments*. A work would end with the note. An additional article follows. It nevertheless remained the last one on the problem. Works that seemed concluded pointed beyond themselves, required more extensive work; something was never finished in the sense of completion. He hardly ever published a book; once there appeared a Roman agrarian history and a booklet about the stock market, and in recent years a few notebook discourses—otherwise nothing.[1] Everything else is in periodicals, archives, newspapers. Less than a year ago Max Weber had begun to reap, as it were, the harvest of his scientific life. He prepared two multivolume works. His capacity for work was extraordinary, despite the passage of long decades. In April 1920 he said, "I work like thirty years ago. . . ."[2] He once wrote an entire booklet in a day. It flowed into him. Death overtook him in his work. Specialized science has lost immeasurably. But his works in progress would probably have remained fragments anyway. They were found in enormous dimensions, like pieces of a medieval cathedral, that could never be finished, in accordance with their nature.

His life in this world was also fragmentary. He was

ready to act when something approached him and put his entire energy into that task, whether it be a judicial proceeding, the execution of a will, or his administration of a military hospital in the first years of the war. In the political world, he began to speak whenever he could attain a desired effect for the nation. However, with all he did, a series of individual acts remain that, compared with his human greatness and with the acts of world figures, may seem few, indeed nothing.

Is it possible, considering this fragmentary character, to perceive Max Weber as the intellectual zenith of his time? It is possible if we are able to see a positive meaning in his fragmentary existence, and if we believe that his greatness, so far as it can be realized, necessarily has a fragmentary character.

Let us first look at the content of his published *scientific* work. It is most diverse: Roman agrarian history; the stock market; farm laborers from the East Elbe; medieval trading companies; the decline of the ancient world; logical-methodological studies; the Russian Revolution; psychophysics of industrial labor; the Protestant ethic and the spirit of capitalism; religious-sociological works referring to China, India, and Jewry; political works dealing with the problems of the selection of leaders and the formation of the will; lectures about politics and science as vocations.[3]

This universality, however, is not a haphazard accumulation of heterogeneous investigations. Everything has a center—*sociology*—that should have been presented systematically in a final work. What is sociology? That definition is no more clear than that of philosophy. Philosophy has been understood again and again as self-knowledge of the human spirit, from the Greek term "know thyself" through to Hegel. Sociology also claims this self-knowledge, to a great extent, as the scientific form that tends to accept self-knowledge in the present world. Max Weber's central question to which we can refer all his religious-sociological investigations is: Why do we have capitalism in the West? This is a question the present world would like to understand. Max Weber admired Marx's materialistic conception of history—the first step in the self-knowledge of capitalism as a scientific discovery—but what he recognized in it he reduced to one factor among many. In November 1918 at the University of Vienna he lectured a positive critique of the materialistic conception of history, showing the other factors in their effect. He made the religious factor above all, a formative and moving factor even of the economic, the subject of an analysis; but he additionally sought all recognizable connections without absolutizing one of them. His sociology was intended to represent the entire complicated system of causal connections. Referring to the whole of human existence, he thus became universal in his consideration. This consideration is an unprecedented union of history and methodology. He quite empirically kept to the endless material and was, however, constructive at every moment from systematic viewpoints, among which everything that is historical becomes a mere "case." The system never became too rigid. On the contrary, Max Weber intentionally stressed everywhere that his distinctions and concept structures were formed for this special purpose for knowledge and claimed no validity beyond that. Even the distinction of value spheres for him became appropriate concept structures for certain knowledge, to be sure, of a very manifold practicability. But even this distinction signified nothing absolute to him.

Is this sociology, then, perhaps philosophy under another name? Max Weber wanted to be a specialized scientist and considered his sociology a specialized science. It is, however, a strange specialized science: It is without its own subject matter because other scientists, who are really merely specialized, already worked on all of it before. A specialized science that becomes universal, as did great philosophy, lets all sciences work for it and fertilizes all sciences—so far as they have something to do with man as an object. Sociology has an external similarity with philosophy in that there is no generally recognized standard, no objective criterion for the scientific value, as in the specialized sciences. The close relationship to philosophy also seems externally visible because official [academic] philosophers have devoted themselves to it. It is just as much a philosophical discipline as the one fostered by political economists. Simmel and Troeltsch[4] are two such contemporary philosophers. Troeltsch, however, admits his debt to Max Weber. Philosophy, wherever it is alive, always has a concrete, rooted base. It grows from individual areas of life and knowledge: from the ethical-political world, mathematical natural science, logic, history, and so on. In the philosophical process there arises at times a whole from which perhaps a new specialized science isolates itself. Sociology is not yet so advanced as to be a mere specialized science. It is still in the primitive state in which all sciences are co-fluent with philosophy. It is therefore such a living and exciting science; it still has a philosophical character. Since it after all is only a root field of philosophy, only knowledge and only a part of knowledge, it thus cannot claim to be philosophy. Max Weber stressed what was scientifically specialized in his work from philosophical conviction; he strove to make sociology a specialized science from scientific conviction. Because sociology is so encompassing and universal, it was just an individual pursuit for him. The philosopher is more extensive.

He found only *one* effect in sociological perception.

A *philosopher* is more than merely a perceiver. The *material* that he perceives and its origin affect him. Time, its movement and its uncertainty, is present in his personality: the forces of time form the most resolute life in unusual brightness. He represents what time is; he is time in a most substantial way, while others only realize parts, variations, depletions, and distortions of temporal forces. The philosopher is not only the heart in the life of time, he is able to express time, to hold the mirror before it and, while expressing it, to determine it intellectually. The philosopher is therefore a human being who is always true to his personality, standing up for himself wherever he sets himself up. If he did not do that, he would lack the material for his most original knowledge; he would only carry out intellectual movements. The knowledge that would then arise would be detached from all existence, representing depleted activity in a vacuum with indifferent matter that presupposes no existence, but is in everyone's hand like worn coinage. We have seen embodied in Max Weber, however, an existential philosopher. While other people essentially know only their personal fate, the fate of time worked creatively in his broad soul. Even though he experienced and shaped the personal element with the power and love of his human heart, all was superimposed by a greater ele-

ment. The macro-anthropoid of our world stood personally before us in him. His striking definitions for
the events and decisions of our time, experienced
deeply by him, fascinated us; through him we
reached the clearest consciousness of the present and
the moment. His clairvoyant glance into the future,
his classifying the present into the total historical
perspective, and, at the same time, his strong consciousness of the sheer vivacity of present existential
tasks, were fascinating. Among these demands past
works, even the great works, could seem like "old
notebooks" to him. He had a current consciousness
of the world and self.

But he did not place it before us in its totality.
With inexorable consistency he seemed only to separate, not unite the complete picture. It is generally
known that he separated, for example, perceiving
and valuing, with some pathos. The goal of science
was for him value-free knowledge. His intellectual
conscience expanded his glance infinitely, while he
incessantly sought to bring his own valuations into
consciousness, making them the subject of knowledge. His requirements for perceiving were seeing,
without illusions, what is real and valid in rational
consequences, and what is a causal factor and what
unavoidably occurs under given conditions. But this
requirement of the separation of valuation and objective insight did not signify indifference to life and

seclusion in an aimless subject, not "death with a wide-awake eye," not a rest cushion of contemplative watching. True seeing was without illusions and at the same time a stimulus for intensive valuation to him. Unity and completion were not his objective form, not even as the personal, empirical, accomplished figure of Max Weber was ours, but as a living movement in his existence that came to instantaneous, completed synthesis. He did not forget objectivity while valuing, or the possible valuations in the case of objective discussion, continually referring successively to what was separated and at the same time to what remained separated in the reference. Thus, what was contrasted in an infinite agitation was united in him!

His limitless objectivity was the reason that he, as hardly a human being of our time, was able to listen to arguments and remain accessible to every fact and argument. If the Greeks were distinguished from the barbarians by the fact that they, in contrast, listened to reason, then Max Weber was a Greek of high rank. His questions and willingness to listen knew no limits. But at the same time, this human being was vehement in valuation, of a determination of the expressed opinion of the concrete events of existence that appeared to many as frightening, brutal, and oppressive. But he was always such, based on insight he never wanted to push aside, and even adhering to the fact that he was not only objective for a limited sphere of scientific work but in everything. His excessive temperament, his anger in the face of insincerity, arrogance, and self-deception probably, at times, penetrated his moderate mental attitude and many thought that they could not deal with him. He shouted everyone down, monopolized entire discussions, and was arrogant and radical. The fact was, his abundant insight and material knowledge was sometimes overwhelming; there were no more objections, at least as far as anyone knew. That his moral demands did not sit comfortably demonstrated that he was a living conscience for everyone who did not completely isolate oneself. While it is also true that his temperament led him to emotional excesses and momentary injustices, it is marvellous how this man admitted doubting of his ability for great tasks demanding frequent, momentary decisions: "I make mistakes." Whatever happened in his momentary emotional state was correctable. His boundless capacity for instructing over the long run proved unfailing for everyone who really had substance and objectivity. Therefore, anyone who had a clear conscience could have absolute confidence in him.

Max Weber declined to be a philosopher if we wished to consider him as such. The whole and the absolute were not subjects for him. He intensively resisted the philosophical system; all the more energetically did he think systematically and constructively in all areas. All his methodology was valid for limited purposes of knowledge for him and, therefore, was of limited relative significance. He was conscious of the percipient difference separating him from philosophy—the systems final goal—and saw in the historical conception (from Hegel to Windelband)[5] that the entire history of philosophy is strangely distorted from this perspective. Max Weber recognized that this conception of history, the vision of the objective connection of logical questions that cast a progressive meaning and an objective problematical development in history into bold relief, was great. But the logical aspect, which should actually have been the single task of this philosophy, was for Max Weber essentially a specialized science that he also studied. Philosophy was logic for him; as a system, however, it was strange to him. He used to say with Socratic irony, "I do not understand anything about it," or declare very calmly that those were quite "other" problems with which he was not occupied. He used these concepts only in their quite definite significance for the analysis of this particular reality. He did not claim to know the ultimate meaning of existence. In his philosophical existence there was, therefore, neither a prophetic belief that could be announced nor a philosophical system that could bestow a world concept as receptacle, consolation, survey, and shelter. Therefore, in his case, the fragmentary, without being directly desired, needed a deep symbolic meaning.

What does *fragmentary* mean? It is partially external fate. Just as death has interrupted work, so did earlier illness[6] cause much to remain unfinished, and ultimately the political structure of Germany in all its forms has kept him from being effective. He interrupted works that were indeed important to him, but that nevertheless lay farther from the center, like purely logical-methodological investigations, investigations about the psychophysics of industrial labor, and the analysis of the first Russian Revolution. He felt himself dependent on others at times in these more peripheral works and stressed these dependencies on Rickert, Kraepelin,[7] and so on, with an almost exaggerated firmness. Max Weber at times, when he investigated a field, abandoned it in mid-course of his impetuously advancing research, after he had surveyed it and done what was necessary for him. For him the central element was sociology. But even here, however, everything had a fragmentary character, even in the infinite expansion and extent of his studies. It is a foundation of his philosophical existence. He is a fragmentarian from a consciousness of totality and the absolute, which can be expressed in no other manner. Man, as a finite being, can only make individual things subject of his will, and can never directly grasp hold of the whole and the absolute—only indirectly, through the clearest separation, the distinct comprehending of the particular. If, in the process, he took the wrong path, with his quite irrational conscience, and with the enthusiasm that at times places his entire being into the individual element, then philosophical existence, which in itself can never be the aim of his will, grows in him and becomes visible for others, never ready, but always in a state of agitated precedence whose documents are those great fragments. The absolute, the unconditional was present to Weber, indeed existentially, with unusual force, not as subject, formula, or content, but as if operating alone in concrete action, temporal situation, and limited perception stressing the specialized. We may say that the whole was in the finite for him, so that the finite seemed to grow from an infinite content. This man sought no system nor completion of work in his demonically restless movement; completion would have narrowed, deluded, and dazzled him. Each individual thing he seized was inflamed so that it had to act as the direct radiation of its absolute, itself remaining in the background. It was not the vehemence merely of a temperament but of the ideas that moved him, letting him storm about from one fragmentary realization to the next. The spirit was in him, something with which he can be alone at full animation in a temporal existence—never a satisfied, active, impetuous movement. This synthesis is something incredible because it is contradictory; nowhere does he seem to possess the absolute as content, and yet he took hold of each subject he grasped with pathos as if it were the absolute. He could appear as the complete relativist—and yet he was the most fervent believer of our time. This belief endured the relativizing of everything that becomes subject for us and is thereby one merely individual element.

If we characterize people by their attachment to typical professions, then the question about Max Weber would be: Was he a *scholar* or a *politician?*

He was a patriot. He believed in Germany under all circumstances. To be sure, he saw realities without illusion; he created no illusions. His relentless, sincere criticism of the fatherland was a criticism born of love. We could never discern more strongly what unconditional patriotism was than by Max Weber's positive conclusion after critical considerations: I thank God that I am a German. This patriotism was the last standard for him and his political will. For him, Germany's welfare did not coincide with the welfare of any class, or with the affirmation of any philosophy, of life, or any special political pattern. Catholic or Protestant, conservative or so-

cialist, monarchical or democratic—these considerations had to take second place when it was a question
of Germany. Therefore he was ready, whenever foreign policy demanded, to go with any party or philosophy of life that promised the greatest success for
the fatherland. All political considerations were for
him, therefore, technical considerations about objectively suitable means, not ideologically based on
principle. Politics for him was not a matter of belief—ideological combatants can only be slayed with
power—but a question of expert knowledge, objectivity, responsibility, and compromise. During the
war he suffered silently—rage and despair were basic
outbursts of his great nature—while witnessing
disadvantageous political stupidity time after time.
When it was possible he began to speak: for parliamentary reform, democratization, and in revolutionary times.[8] His courage to candidly speak what he
saw and believed was equally great whether he opposed the top powers of the old state or the workers.
When he said uncomfortable things to the workers
in public meetings and rage stormed against him, we
saw how a great man can work creatively. Despite
opposition, his figure commanded respect. His veracity and also the deep earnestness and love for people
had to be believed, and he was able to succeed. The
listeners felt themselves addressed with a profundity
that no one else attained. He was fully involved in

political thought and, aware of his specialized knowledge, was always prepared to use his ability and knowledge politically if called. We could easily conclude that he was a politician who did not become important due to adversity. Nevertheless, something quite essential distinguished him from the genuine "born" politician. Max Weber was not ready to seize power by himself, to use any means used today, as always—as diverse as they might be—to attain power. He was ready if called and needed, not of his own initiative, to seek leadership and shape his fatherland from the consciousness of his profession. No true politician and statesman can feel this way. He wants power; it is a condition of his existence. Max Weber could live without it, like the Platonic philosopher who is only ready to govern the state out of duty.

If he were really not a politician, as we probably agree, Max Weber was a *scholar* according to his nature. He did research from the purest disinterested drive for knowledge. He had the strongest awareness of the methods and types, and how validity is established by knowledge and within what limits. He dominated the technical mechanism of the scientific trade. In the critical interpretation of scientific accomplishments, he was incorruptible. Perhaps he was so often disappointed in people whenever he saw their scientific works, that he probably never conveyed any of his illusions to judging their scientific value. If, however, Max Weber was a scholar of first rank, then he was also an expert politician. He was both, but both were not his ultimate nature. He was not essentially a scholar because he lacked the specialized scientific limitation that proceeds, step by step, in splendid self-restraint, infinite patience, and an absolute lifetime mastery of a field. Attitudinally, he was neither a philologist nor an experimenting natural scientist, although he possessed a lively sense for both and occasionally not only used their results but also practiced them for a time. His will for knowledge was more universally directed, and had, with mastery of the matter, something of the impetuous. He used results of individual sciences in his new sociological formulations of questions much more than even a specialized science. Everywhere he worked well with sources, e.g. learned Russian with astonishing rapidity in order to follow the newspapers and writings of the first Russian Revolution. But they were only moments initiating additional rapid writings intended to lead him to self-knowledge of the present. He did not always feel comfortable in the process because he regarded working in specialized science as substantial in itself; therefore his writings are permeated with emphasis on his dependencies and the relative validity of the experimental nature of his works. He probably had an instinctive aversion for the fact that his type of investigations could be imitated by inadequate means, for he was aware of having even the specialized scientific basis and nevertheless still accomplishing the problematical. Most of what goes by the name sociology appeared fraudulent to him.

Neither politics nor scholarship was of central, absolute importance for Max Weber. The facility with which he gave up one in order to devote himself to the other was astounding. At the time of the revolution, he passionately began to speak out of national interest. When his candidacy for election to the National Assembly was impeded, at the last moment, within the democratic parties, he resigned without resentment or animosity; then when his candidacy in the National Assembly was tempestuously demanded against the will of the leaders, he admonished party discipline and declared that he was not irreplaceable. When the military hospital administration was taken away from him in the second year of the war, he was for a moment somewhat sad not to be performing a service for the fatherland, but the next day he zealously resumed his religious-sociological studies. He renounced these again with a memorandum,[9] hoping to help prevent unlimited submarine warfare. The rapidity with which he passed from one to the other was surprising. He gave the same intensity to everything. At any given time anything could be his profession; he nevertheless was able to forego each activity. We would misunderstand him completely if we were to think that he was basically indifferent to everything. The marvelous quality this man had was that he took up with complete seriousness, with an unconditional pathos, that which he generally took up; he somehow still stood behind it with his deepest being. We could say that his activity accompanied a complete awareness: Everything is nothing before God, but it is our essence to create meaning, to fulfill tasks; otherwise we are empty. Unconcerned with what may finally result and dominated by the knowledge of the recurring destruction of all values that we realize in this world, his activity was just all the more heroically increased.

He, moreover, attached no importance at all to his person, not even to merely speak of it. If it was in danger of being destroyed by hostile bombs or Bolshevism or sickness, he was indifferent because sensation lay outside the activity of his will. Death or any other fate did not frighten him. He was deeply moved by events; he was desperate over Germany's collapse to the point of even wanting to perish himself. And yet, with all this passionate experiencing and first-hand witnessing, something in him was unshakeable. By nothing more could he be reduced to complete despair, but he might have been incapable merely of vital strength or weak resignation. Rather, by preserving all natural lively emotions, with a clairvoyant glance at reality, he was concurrently in another timeless world.

What was he? He, himself, had no answer to that and knew none. He was no stoic because apathy and formal peace of mind were so little his or even aspired to by him; rather, their opposites lived in him. But, in his self-sufficiency and solitary unshakeableness, he had some of the stoic's omniscence.

He was also no Christian. For him, to be a Christian was to accept the commandment of the Sermon on the Mount: do not succumb to evil. He did not want to fulfill this commandment because it was incompatible with operating in the world. He had respect for the genuine realization of this conviction, but one could feel him drawing back as he spoke of the unworthiness in which this commandment may result. Whenever he talked about self-deceptions in theodicy and its experiments, he often became bitingly ironic. Sometimes his words could sound like blasphemy. Arising from deep veracity, there was a rejection of belief that obscures and has a calming effect on reality. This rejection did not come from cynicism nor indifferent skepticism, but from a terribly serious awareness of an inexpressible, incomprehensible absolute. His work regarding the Protestant ethic and the spirit of capitalism, as "value free," direct, and objective as is it, tells us almost indirectly how Max Weber stood in relation to Christianity. In this work, an unprecedented tension of opposite, unexpressed possibilities of valuation lies hidden. No religiousness on earth stood so close to his heart as this puritanical sect. The impenetrable decree of God—predestination—suited his strict meaning and his veracity, which leaves the impenetrable unpenetrated. But he was far from attaching himself inwardly to this religious world. He saw this grand phenomenon as having effects, under the guidance of initially effective religious power, that must have appeared terribly contradictory to him. Should the grandest, most serious, and most heroic human phenomena bring about disaster, emptiness, and intellectual death?

What was Max Weber, if he was neither simply a politician nor merely a specialized scholar, neither a stoic nor a Christian, in the ideological sense? If we answer that he was a philosopher, then he was not a philosopher even in the sense he believed himself. He gave a new fulfillment to the idea of the philosopher, for what a philosopher may be is not abstract and generally definable. He provided actual character with philosophical existence. In him we could see what was now a philosopher if we doubted whether there were still philosophers at all. The essence of a philosophical existence, in any case, is being aware of the absolute, dealing with it, and an approach that

is unconditionally supported by the kinetic seriousness of the absolute. Max Weber's unique quality
was this essence that radiated from him, without his
recognizing and showing the absolute objectively.

If we, after all, want to look for formulas improp-
erly in order to grasp the content of such a philosophical existence, at its center, then we can only
find such formulas of a predominantly negative character. Max Weber believed in the possibility of *freedom* and demanded that others be willing to be free.
He refused to be a prophet and leader; he was indeed
hypersensitive on this point because he realized his
extraordinarily personal action was a danger. He felt
himself a human and rational being and wished that
others were also, of their own accord. He, therefore,
did not like intellectual and ideological subordina-
tion to an authoritative nature that was ready to rule
whenever people came together for a cause. He,
therefore, loved every evidence of self-reliance, however slight, he loved disagreement and struggle, and
he demanded to be confronted on the same level. To
be sure, he never meant by this the particular empirical individuality; for him, this was immaterial, and
when he saw how others wanted to fully live their
particular individuality, to say something special,
something possible only for them, he endured it with
difficulty. Freedom to him was the medium for the

growth of something above the personal: the idea, the spirit, the subject—he preferred the last word. He avoided sensation as much as possible in action and speech and sought to stay with what was limited, with the special tasks, not expressing himself about the ultimate, probably knowing such expressions would be used as slogans and formulas and that he would be made a prophet. He did not want to be a prophet, and he rejected prophets everywhere. Even though the spirit alone was existential for him in personalities, he himself never perceived a single human being, dead or living, as his leader or hero, either in his youth or later. He possessed the most vivacious view of human personalities. Individuals like Cromwell and Kant possessed his special favor, others, like Bismarck and Fichte, despite the respect and admiration they received from others, his disfavor.[10]

Whatever Max Weber may be cannot be determined if we read one of his works, and still less if we read a few formulas about him; it can be determined in the entirety of the fragments—the scientific works, articles, newspaper pieces, memoranda, letters, literary remnants, and in addition, modest amorphous reports about his life, actions, and behavioral habits. A unity becomes indubitable in the entirety of these sonorous fragments, not formulated and rational, but clearly present: the idea of this philosophical existence. In the present world, he has, nevertheless, demonstrated this idea, absolute and general and timeless as it may be in its ultimate depth, in a special original phenomenon.

In him the spirit has become the bright flame. Now there only remains to guard the glowing sparks that slumber in us, in every human being. In Max Weber's view of being, these sparks can glow a little brighter.

The idea of his philosophical existence is, like all great things lately, a secret. But for us, it is the living source and task of a philosophy that does not want to be reproductive, romantic, or of empty timelessness, but present and solely conscious of the eternal in a present, temporal form. Our time appears to many as merely confused, relativistic, beliefless, intellectual, and industrious. And some find no outlet other than a romantic flight into the forgotten or even an industrious restoration of past patterns of life. He who considers it possible, however, that everything criticized in the present-day world may be peripheral phenomenon, depletion, and degeneration of the substantial, and believes that every epoch contains the presence of the eternal, is able to see in Max Weber a substantial phenomenon of our time. We recognize him in the life-creating impulse that emanates to us. His presence made us aware that, even today, the spirit could exist in forms of the highest degree. Because we saw him, we believed only rightly the dimension of the great dead known to us only as historical human beings. We see him now in their realm as a man of equally high birth.

Max Weber:
Politician,
Scientist,
Philosopher

(1932)

Preface (1958)

M ax Weber (1864–1920) was the greatest German of our era. Such a judgment anticipates what only subsequent periods can determine with finality. I dare to express it, despite it's being impermissible. I have lived with this conviction for almost half a century.

This work on Max Weber, which can only hint at his greatness, was first published in 1932 and is now being reprinted unchanged. At the time of its first publication, amid the onset of National Socialism, it was supposed to be a reminder of the truth possible in Germany. The great man was bound to be invoked against the confusion. He wanted to sensibly communicate our own claims against Germandom [culture and nationality] falsified at that time.

Max Weber is represented here as a politician, scientist, and philosopher. Politics, only a moment in his life, was always passionately grasped by him and brought to consciousness. For us today, the contents of his politically active thinking are still primarily only of a historical character, although of the greatest interest to Germans. He was the last national German. His point of departure was a powerful German Empire and his experiences of a powerful German Empire, defeated in World War I, and struggling with its reconstruction. Today, all politics is conducted under new historical assumptions that lay outside horizons thought practically possible by Max Weber. Through Weber we are reminded of a past, irrevocably destroyed, in which he took paths that were rejected by Germany. His political conviction, however, is everlasting. He understood the only course possible for us in a democracy, but he clairvoyantly espied the democracy's enormous dangers, overcome only when knowledge of them is disseminated throughout the nation. He felt the severity of reality, the greatness of responsibility, the breath of sinister world history. To an important Swiss who said, conversationally, "We must love the state!" he replied: "What, we must love the monster in spite of everything!"[1]

Max Weber, sociologist and historian, is imperishable for the world. His scientific achievements lie before us in powerful works. As with Galileo, substantive recent discoveries are connected with the most lucid, methodological awareness. Just as the latter did in the natural sciences, so Max Weber has done in his final step, quite different here, in the humanities for pure science, not only in philological and other preliminary works long since known, but in the subject itself. Coming to this perception is difficult: his work in its precise and very extensive abstractness is avoided like a granite block upon which we do not like to climb. Its influence has only begun to be felt, above all, in America, but also in England, France, and Germany. He has elevated sociology from common idle talk, cheap banality, and speculative folly to a science, and one could say reluctantly: Most of what goes by the name of sociology is fraudulent.

This world, rich in experience, knowledge, and unprecedented research methods is held together by Weber's personality. He always spoke of his subject; only reluctantly did he speak of himself. He did not mirror himself in reflection. He was there in his truthfulness, therefore, in his pure scientific method, sustained by a powerful passion not easily controlled. He was prone to occasional excesses, however, but these he was generally able to correct. His great heart was omnipresent. His ethical intransigence remained free of fanaticism. Although this personality can only be fully evident to those who met him personally, it is felt in his work, through the philosophy which, though only seldom explicitly mentioned, encompasses everything.

His existence was an encouragement for all who proceed into the future without illusions, who remain active as long as it is possible to do so, and who maintain hope as long as all is not lost. He was the modern human being who permitted no concealment, who finds in this veracity life's impetus, allowing no escape into despair. Like reason itself, he was fulfilled and reclaimed from the great disquiet before the onrushing currents of history and the emotional turmoil of his life.

Introduction

We contemplate, in the form of historical realization, what people can be; they open for us the scope
of possiblities in which we live. But each individual
historical figure is remote to us because we did not
experience the times in which he or she lived. Contemporaries who shared with us the common fate,
who spoke personally to us, are our reality, from
which we acquire, in a unique way, the standard by
which we see distant and strange humanity.

In Germany, in the years before and during the
world war, many saw human greatness embodied in
Max Weber; they believed in, were oriented by, and,
above all, loved him with that love which uplifts us
and causes what is real in us to grow.

It is a task to preserve for posterity a view of this
side of the recent past and still present German
essence that, although only slightly visible to us, is all
the more effective in the secret soul of the German

people. This is the essence of real rationality and humanity, with passion as its origin.

Max Weber was born in 1864, studied law, and was a professor of political economy from 1894–97 at Freiburg and from 1897–99 at Heidelberg, where he retired to recuperate from a neurosis. As a captain in the reserves, he volunteered for military service and administered the Heidelberg military hospital in the first years of the war. In 1919 he took over Brentano's[2] professorial chair at the University of Munich. Well-known and respected among his colleagues as an enlightened person, he was, nevertheless, scarcely known to the general public when he died unexpectedly of pneumonia in June 1920, at the age of fifty-six.

What he really was is not self-evident. His position and his volumes of works show that he was a *scientist.* But he was not exclusively and ultimately that; he talked about his activity as a lecturer reluctantly although he had a charming effect on an audience. In spite of the power and richness of his scientific oeuvre, he did not, for some reason, seem to find this endeavor important.

He passionately pursued political events all his life, reacted to them and spoke his mind. Towards the end of the war and the subsequent collapse of Germany, following the revolt of the masses, he was publicly prominent for awhile. Whatever he said about the respective political situation was strikingly to the point. If for this reason, we were to think that he was really a *politician* who did not become important due to fate and circumstances, his greatness could only have been that of a Raphael without arms; this was a potential.

Neither his political activity nor his individual scientific accomplishments—impressive and mighty as they are—were the reason he occupies such a unique position in the hearts of some Germans: Max Weber was the richest and deepest realization of the meaning of floundering in our time. He took upon himself the entire range of German culture and lived in a German state when both were already in ruin; he did it with a soul that not only suffered from it but was brought to brightness by what was happening—not generally from a calm objective skepticism, but particularly from a belief offering resistance and reality even in hopeless situations, despite everything. He actively fulfilled his being in an era of decline. He was a *philosopher* because he accomplished this, although unintentionally, and as fate would have it it became clearly visible through insight, word, and action. Being a philosopher is not always the same thing at all times, but something new and original for every age. What is common is simply that the philosopher is also what he knows; that he is the brightness of an unconditional being.

The being of another that does not understand itself in its dullness can come to itself through him. Max Weber's work is a unique expression of this concrete philosophizing entirely arising on its own from within which takes place in the medium of political judgment and scientific investigation, just as his life was a unique philosophizing in the medium of his existence.

If Max Weber was a politician, scientist, and philosopher, then he was, nevertheless, not merely one and also the other, but the whole human being who grasped the world in an unprecedented vastness from the depths of his being, which, indivisibly *one*, is really what a human being as a human being can be: a seeker of truth. As a philosopher, he is a politician; as a philosopher, he is a scientist.

Max Weber as a Politician

M ax Weber did not become a leading statesman; he remained a political writer. But although he did not act, he lived in constant readiness. His thinking was in every fiber the reality of a political human being, an operating political will serving the historical moment.

Nevertheless, political truth and political deed are separated by a leap. It often happened in history that insight was powerless and became only a legacy for posterity. A glance at Max Weber's attitude towards the situations and events during his life leads to questions: Why did he remain without influence? What would have happened if he had come to leadership? What is the lasting claim of his political thinking?

The Struggle against the System

Even in his youth, when Germany lived in the radiance of Bismarck, whose events Max Weber experienced through contact with the national liberal uncommitted politicians in his paternal home in Berlin, he was *indeterminately apprehensive.* He admired Bismarck, but saw with alarm "the terrible destruction of independent conviction that Bismarck wrought in us. . . ."[3] At that time, he deplored "the treacherous gift of Bismarckian Caesarism: universal suffrage. . . .,"[4] which indeed may not mean equal rights for all in the true sense of the word. He repudiated what was current at that time throughout society: "the worship of the militaristic and other lack of consideration, the culture of so-called realism and the Philistine contempt for all the aspirations of those who hope to attain their goal without appeal to the baser aspects of people, particularly brutality. . . ."[5] He could not sanction the *Kulturkampf* [Bismarck's struggle with Roman Catholicism] or its mode of disengagement. To him peace, unheralded and unsung, was an admission of injustice. If we say the struggle had only political grounds from Bismarck's point of view, if it were therefore, not a matter of conscience but only one of opportunity, then the conscience of the Catholic people was ravished; it had not been conscience against conscience.

cal thought revolved around this one point. From time to time, in a concrete situation such as in 1906 and 1908, he tried to open the eyes of those accessible to him—even if only in private letters. All those informed, as well as top-ranking military personnel, seemed to be in agreement regarding the emperor; each told the other: Wherever he intervenes, he produces disaster. It was also clear to many what Max Weber said: The monarch was not a decisive factor. Every hereditary monarch was a political dilettante unless he was, by chance, a Frederick the Great. The system is the decisive factor. It was known that the German political constitution was a hollow constitutionalism. But Max Weber struggled against this not perhaps on grounds of natural law or doctrine, not because of political freedom in itself, but on the grounds of national power and honor. To him this system demonstrated the fault of the political inability of leading men. Indeed, Bismarck once arose as an exception, who simultaneously completed this system as an instrument of his power; but Weber also thought it possible that Bismarck—without resistance—tolerated only creatures without character around himself, and so after his departure, following a period of decades, there was simply no successor. To Max Weber, everything depends on how true statesmen become controllers of the rudder of state in a constitutional monarchy; only then

"We therefore acted *without conscience* and are even morally the losers, and that is the bitterest part of defeat. . . ."[6] The fact that ethical demoralization and insincerity increased in the time of Bismarck precluded the young man's expectation of anything good for the future.

As an adult, Max Weber voted conservatively and joined the Pan-German League. In his political view, everything depended upon *the life and power of the German people*. He soon saw that that league put the great landowners' interest in cheap Polish labor before the national interest of the permanent German peasantry, and thereupon resigned. *After the dismissal of Bismarck,* when the emperor catastrophically endangered Germany with his political dilettantism, and reduced it to impotence in world politics, the Conservative Party, in the power interests of the classes constituting it, shielded *the system* in which alone such a dangerous monarchical drive was possible. Weber became the embittered opponent of this party which, in his view, was risking the nation's future.

Max Weber saw early the *path into the political abyss* now taken. His apprehension was definite: "The politics of Europe are no longer made in Berlin."[7] "As if by a miracle are we still now evading really serious diplomatic situations."[8] From then to the outbreak of the world war, Max Weber's politi-

could the nation pursue world politics and preserve itself from catastrophe.

Whether, with a modified system, statesmen would arise from among the people, becomes the vital question.

Even in 1895 in his academic inaugural address,[9] Weber questioned *where* political leaders should come from. He asked about the political maturity of the *classes;* that is, their ability to put the enduring economic and political interests of the nation above all other considerations. This political standard of value was the sovereign standard of the classes for him, but he did not think he would find this maturity anywhere.

The *Junkers* who led us up till now would no longer sieze the task in world politics. It was dangerous and, in the long run, incompatible with the nation's interests if an economically declining class should control political leadership. Certainly the strength of the political instincts of the *Junker* class was one of the most powerful assets that could be used in the service of the power of the state, but now they lay in an economic death struggle from which no economic policy could restore them to their old social character. Even the tasks of the present were different from those they could solve. For a quarter of a century the last and greatest of the *Junkers* had stood at the helm of Germany, and the tragedy was that he irrevocably changed the economic structure of the nation to which he gave unity. In the final analysis, this had induced the partial floundering of Bismarck's life's work, for it should have led not only to the exterior, but also to the inner unification of the nation, and that has not been attained.

Max Weber, at that time, regarded the other classes, for whom the expectation of political rule was moving with economic power, as politically immature. If he talked about the bourgeoisie, he exhibited increasing wrath that Bismarck's creation of the German bourgeoisie, a class drunk with success and thirsting for peace, had engendered an apolitical spirit. Perhaps he lamented the silent decline in mid-century of the political upper bourgeoisie that had left most of its great figures politically anonoymous. Now the composition of the bourgeoisie was different. Since German history seemed to him at an end with the fulfillment of the past millennium, it seemed for the satiated class as if modesty forbade world history from returning to the agenda of its daily routine after the successes of the German nation. Max Weber fluctuated between this anger at the cowardice of the bourgeoisie who longed only for a new Caesar or lapsed into philistinism, and his rage at Bismarck who helped bring about this development. "The powerful sun which was at the zenith of Germany and caused the German name to shine in the most remote corners of the earth was, so it almost seems, too big for us and has burned out the slowly developing political discernment of the bourgeoisie."[10]

There remained to ask, after the failure of the *Junkers* and the bourgeoisie, whether the *working class* would produce leaders who would seize the world political helm. But this class seemed just as innocuous as it was immature to Max Weber in 1895: ". . . no spark of that Catilinarian energy of action . . ."[11] was in it as in the men of the French Revolution. It lacked the great instincts of power.

Realizing this situation, Weber thought: "We must understand that the unification of Germany was a youthful prank which the nation committed in its old age and by reason of its costliness would have been better left undone, if it were to be the conclusion and not the starting point of a German world power politics."[12] Even the purpose of socio-political work, therefore, may not be prosperity, but the social unification of the nation, which may be disrupted by modern economic development, for the difficult struggles of the future. Were it possible to create a workers' aristocracy that would represent a political conviction, "only then might the spear, for which the arm of the bourgeoisie still does not seem to grow strong enough, be placed on those broader shoulders."[13] The development of a national political sense in leaders of workers may be the decisive

element, for Max Weber sees the "illusion of independent 'social-political' ideals . . ."[14] disappearing
before the great questions of world power politics.

In a situation appearing doubly disconsolate—the
classes that could provide state leaders were not
decisively visible, and the *system,* necessarily wrong,
that did not bring statesmen, perhaps arising from
the people to leadership—Max Weber saw the danger of Germany's decline abroad as the sole essential
element. Perhaps few have so definitely thought of
impending disaster, as Max Weber did, in a period
of national prosperity. To prevent decline at the last
moment, he decided in favor of a *parliamentarianism*
sketched since 1917 in his essays[15] as the only possible path *for the selection* of political leaders. From
1917 his urging for immediate domestic action has
been continuous. Everything, foreign and domestic,
depends upon correct and immediate action. Max
Weber advocated a democracy on whose trust the
statesman is so dependent that he rules authorita-
tively, supported by this trust, but bears the real
responsibility through personal danger, with liability
to the people, who may perhaps demand his head.
For Max Weber, the question of a political constitution is solely a question of technique, not philosophical outlook. He asks about the effect of a national
power that can be secured only by the superior intel-
ligence of statesmen. He is certain that only a gov-

ernment supported by the people can bring the nation's power to its highest intensity. The decisive question of his political thinking, therefore, is how the inevitable democracy with the authoritative leadership of truly competent and responsible statesmen can subsist in living harmony. During the war and subsequent collapse arose the series of great political writings in which he carefully thought out, in detail, what to him was pertinent to the moment, but which remains doctrine forever.

More than twenty years elapsed between Max Weber's first clairvoyant glance and the outbreak of the great war which befell Germany in its politically committed isolation, and for the present put an end to her as a world power. Throughout these years Max Weber, despite his powerlessness due to illness and his office, tried to speak out again and again in situations of domestic politics; change, after all, could be possible. For example, in 1906, when the *Reichstag* was dissolved because the Catholic Center Party and the Social Democratic Party had rejected the emperor's colonial budget, Max Weber sought to make clear to the liberals that their campaign platform must in no way become a vote of confidence for the emperor; rather, the platform would have to be directed against the Center Party not only because of the rejection of the colonial budget, but also because this party may not want the real power of the Parliament against the government, but only public office patronage. Bringing statesmen to the pinnacle and eliminating the extravagances of a politically incapable monarch may depend upon Parliament's power. "The measure of contempt which is gradually shown to us abroad. . . . as a nation—and rightly so! that is the decisive element—because we tolerate this regime of this man, has gradually become a power factor of first class 'world political' significance for us. . . . We are becoming 'isolated'. . . ."[16]

Max Weber and the German Collapse

For two decades Max Weber's political thinking followed one and the same objective. What he thought is infinitely simple; putting it into action, infinitely difficult. He could see the decisive reason for the German fate but could not change it. The government did not seek him; the masses would not have followed him if he could have been a leader.

When the war broke out in 1914, Max Weber was passionately aroused. What he had been predicting for two decades happened but he had always considered it avoidable, and still did. The military victories in a situation that to all non-Germans had seemed lost for Germany strengthened his hope but did not distort his view. Even in Germany's moment of greatest military superiority, he only considered possible a peace without European annexations; Germany's mere self-assertion in this situation would mean the greatest victory, incomparably elevating Germany's world prestige. He opposed the politics of greed in favor of objectively possible, attainable demands; he opposed the "politics of aplomb" in favor of a reasonable diplomacy, effective through tone; he opposed demagogical agitation for intensified submarine warfare in favor of the sole responsibility of the leaders; he opposed the excessive promises [of the war bulletins] in favor of cool, candid portrayal of the situation. In every case, his struggle proceeded against the political stupidity that caused us to lose what would have been possible to attain.

Weber's pessimism never becomes despondency—only the fearful person lives on propaganda that he demands for himself and others—but rather, is the veracity to think of everything that could favorably guide the course of events. His overwhelming belief in Germany only becomes fully apparent in the collapse, then, indeed, with an indeterminate content.

Even as intensified submarine warfare was declared and America's entry into the war became certain, Max Weber saw the turning point: "I suffer less now than all the twenty-five years during which I saw the hysterical vanity of this monarch ruining everything that was sacred and dear to me. 'Fate' has now become that of which human stupidity was previously quite guilty. And we can manage with 'fate.' "[17]

When large sections of the people were fleeing from one illusion to another after the long insincere rousing of sentiment in the collapse, after "Ludendorff's[18] insane gamble when reaction [followed] this 'revolution' . . ."[19] he knew that a new order, perhaps a result of this terrible defeat and disgrace, would not easily take root. He spoke of the revolution as of a kind of narcotic and detested "the many verbosities and . . . the vague hopes and dilettantish frivolities with a 'happier future,'. . ."[20] he turned against the political masochism of an undignified pacifism that wallows voluptuously in guilt feelings "as if military *success* intrinsically might demonstrate something like divine judgement, and as if the god of battles were not 'with the larger battalions' *(we* have shown: not *always!)*. . . ."[21] In 1919 it really seemed to him that everything that defined the greatness of the nation had crashed; he believed he would see the moral forlorness of these people. The nation had bowed to an emperor who was an undignified dilettante; now it considered the bloody carnival of the collapse to be a revolution and was still proud. These people were now hurrying to Versailles, just to be present, whereas every German would have to try to disassociate himself from these negotiations and scenes; the simple decency once possessed seemed lost. Even among those who had made the political and military mistakes, the consequences of which these people had endured for four years with unparalled strength, there were such people who continued to reproach this crushed nation for having made victory impossible by a treacherous stab in the back or in cowardly failure. Max Weber spoke thusly with deep horror when he returned from Versailles, where the government had sent him to form an opinion concerning the acceptance or rejection of the conditions, and his collaboration on a note concerning the question of guilt. He, who in a moment of truthfulness saw nothing more either in the upper or the lower classes, understood: What came to be was too much for the people; it was inhuman to make accusations.

Max Weber, without agreeing with those who believed in a socialist future, saw Germany's future in the *German people.* His love for the Germans had been realized since the beginning of the war as he witnessed the unpretentious bravery of those pulling out and the decent disposition of those returning; in spite of all the dreadfulness experienced he now saw the modest objectivity of the simple people from the trade unions and soldiers whom he got to know in the Heidelberg Workers' and Soldiers' Council. The nation as such, after all, was a disciplined people; we have seen all its weaknesses, but also all its prowess and capacity for the " 'beauty of everyday life,' in contrast to the beauty of intoxication or the balms of others. . . ."[22] "One hundred and ten years ago we showed the world that we—and only we—were capable of being under the foreign domination of one of the quite great civilised peoples. We are doing that once again!"[23] He can be repetitious in new figures of speech: "For I believe in the indestructibility of this Germany and never have I felt being a German so much as a gift of fate as in these dark days of its shame."[24] When he glanced into remote spaces of time, he said, Germany is the only nation to which history twice granted a new youth, after the complete collapses of 1648 and 1806. It will have a third youth after the icy night through which it must now stride.

The German Mission in World History

For the young Max Weber, the establishment of the empire in 1871 was the decisive state of affairs pointing to the future. For Weber a world historical mission lay in it, but it seemed that no one seized it. This mission for Weber was not that of power unfolding, but that which gives consciousness to mind and duty: The preservation of European culture "between the regulations of Russian officials on the one hand, and the conventions of Anglo-Saxon 'society' on the other. . . ."[25] For this task only, German power was a world historical necessity.

The meaning of the world war, for him, was this historical task imposed through the establishment of the empire. "If we did not want to risk this war," he wrote in 1916

well, then we could have discontinued the establishment of the empire indeed and continued to exist as a nation of petty states. . . . Even then we would have had the war: The one confederation might have fought as a confederation of Rhine states for French interests, the other as a Russian satrapy for Russian interests or instead of that, might have given up the theatre of operations. The solemnity of a *German* war, we would not have become acquainted with that. That we are now, as matters stand, not a people of seven but seventy million, *that* was our fate. That inescapable responsibility before history established that. . . . The impetus of this fate which we must meet launched the nation. . . . into a steep trajectory of honour and fame from which there was no return, into the clear air of the governing of world history into whose furious but powerful face it dared and had to gaze; for posterity an immortal memory.[26]

Asked for the definite meaning, however, of German world power, Weber repeated that it meant the decision concerning the individuality of future culture. It should not be passively divided up between Anglo-Saxon conventions and Russian bureaucratic regulations. Posterity would hold not the Danes, Swiss, Dutch, or Norwegians responsible for it, but us. Our duty before posterity was to intervene against the inundation of the entire world by those two powers.

Weber, however, saw the greater danger in *Russia* all the time. England and France could not *permanently* annihilate our existence as a nation and great power, he thought in 1916. For geographical and national political reasons, Russia is the only power that can threaten us, and indeed in increasing measure. After the collapse of Germany in 1918, he therefore became aware, in view of the very unpleasant Anglo-Saxon world domination, that

much that is worse—*Russian* tyranny!—*we* have averted. This glory remains with us. America's world domination was as inevitable as Rome's in antiquity after the Punic War. Hopefully, it *persists*, that it is not shared with Russia. *This,* for me, is the aim of our future world politics, for the Russian danger is only exorcised for now, not forever.[27]

In 1895, Weber had concluded his pessimistic inaugural address: "We will not succeed in banishing the curse under which we stand: To be posthumous to a politically great time—for it would have to be that we would understand becoming something else: precursors of a greater one. Will that be our place in history?"[28] The answer was received in 1918. But Weber does not concede it as final. Our tasks have become smaller with the shattering of our world power, but their actual meaning is there again for him in indeterminate form. He did not predict how this form is molded, but he did not deny his belief in it. The progress of German history remained for him a yet unfulfilled possibility until the end.

Soundness of Political Judgment in Concrete Situations

The prerequisite for political action is a clear vision of what needs to be done at the moment. The simple element on which it depends is concealed by matters of minor importance going astray amidst the many reflections about the reasons for this and that, and in the innumerable viewpoints of the present in which one is already lost without being there. Thinking in a political situation is the grasping of the simple element that can and must be done, like a firm handshake. No one understands the complicated and the complex; we are at a deadlock there. The simple element is indeed the result of complex thinking, but as a result it can be understood by everyone and spur appropriate action. When it was perceived by everyone, it is what they all expected. It was Max Weber's fate to know this simple element from the first on repeated occasions, and to express it at the right time, but to be unheard until later, when everyone understood it, sometimes very quickly, but too late. A few examples of this: The end of 1915, when Germany had its greatest military victories and England had not yet introduced general conscription, was, as we know today, perhaps the single possible moment for Germany to conclude peace. If this was possible, it was possible only if Germany did not intend to annex a square meter. Max Weber sought to bring his view to bear by writing and conversing with those he met, since public discussion of war aims was still forbidden at the time. But results were wanted from the war in Germany, and this peace was called a peace of renunciation. Soon thereafter this opportunity was finally lost.

Between early 1916, when the *Lusitania* was

sunk, and early 1917, when intensified submarine warfare put America on the side of Germany's enemies, Max Weber repeatedly expressed the significance of America's entry into the war in memoranda and letters.[29] He so clearly demanded that necessary and precise accountability for the submarine warfare decision be determined by personal responsibility that every prudent listener should have understood it.

After Germany offered the armistice and the public knew of the Entente's [Britain, France, Russia and their allies] demand imposing complete disarmament upon Germany as a condition of the armistice, when people were talking of a thousand other matters, Max Weber wrote,

There is no doubt among understanding people in Germany about President Wilson's sincerity. It seems, however, that he does not take enough notice of the following: If his wish is complied with that the German government is supposed to accept such armistice conditions that make further military resistance impossible, then, thereby, not only perhaps Germany, but also, on a larger scale, he himself would be eliminated from the series of factors decisive for the conditions of peace. His position as an arbiter depended on and depends on and only on the fact that German military power at least means

KARL JASPERS ON MAX WEBER

so much, since it in no way can be forced into submission without the assistance of American troops. If this were otherwise, the absolutely intransigent elements in the remaining enemy states would gain the upper hand and would be in a position to push the president smoothly aside with polite thanks for his help up to now. His role would be played out. . . .[30]

Indeed, we read a newspaper report documenting the great impression this article had made in North America. But although it was the simplest matter, and could easily be understood, it was America in the person of Wilson that did not act accordingly, resulting in Wilson actually being pushed aside at Versailles, and America, as a belligerent power, a no longer with a weighty word to throw into the balance.

Immediately after the offer of armistice, Max Weber began to write to all those accessible to him on 11 October 1918: The emperor must abdicate. "If he goes now, without pressure from the outside, he will go in honor. . . . the position of the dynasty will be safeguarded. . . . I frankly admit having observed his manner of governing with marked distaste. But in the interest of the empire, I must not wish an emperor to end *in dishonor*. . . ."[31] As a monarchist Weber wanted the abdication, otherwise, the dynasty "which we, nevertheless, wish to preserve"[32] would be impaired. If the emperor were even now to refuse, only to yield afterwards under coercion, repercussions would last for generations. Weber proposed how this must be made clear to the emperor. He would not have to confess guilt, but simply declare: Fate was against me; I abdicate because I wish to make the path easier for the German nation. The response to this proposal was feeble. "Up till now, everyone agrees with me, but no one has the courage to draw the conclusions."[33] Not long after that the enemy demanded the abdication of the emperor; he fled across the border to the Netherlands.

When the enemies' demand for the surrender of our military leaders was imminent, Weber opined: These people, anticipating the demand, would now have to voluntarily surrender to the enemy at a regular international court. This heroic act would give an ethical impetus to the German nation; moreover, the enemy would suffer the greatest embarrassment. He wrote to Ludendorff; the letter led to a personal discussion with negative results.[34]

Political Ineffectiveness

Max Weber's memoranda, essays, and letters are recommendations, insights, reflections, but not deeds. The question is, was his political clairvoyance, which was almost always confirmed by subsequent events, perhaps the expression of his political ability?

Friends indeed believed, whenever they heard him, that this man must lead us. Increasingly during the war, and more ardently during the revolution, they often wished that he would do everything to seize the reins.

He seemed ready, but only if *called*. He did not reach for power. He did not have the politician's innate will for power, the wish to rule because this defines his life. Only in Germany's worst moments did his readiness increase to a positive will, but he waited even then. Noncommittally called to Berlin by political friends, he did not go. ". . . I will only come to Berlin if they want something of me, not merely to sit around and prevaricate."[35]

Sometimes it could seem as if perhaps his instinct unconsciously arranged matters in such a way as to prevent his rise to leadership. But in 1919, for example, he was truly ready for election to the National Assembly and suffered painfully when the German Democratic Party functionaries prevented it. Once in 1917, when a friend asked him why he did nothing to be politically of use to the government, he quite definitely expressed his unwillingness: A politician must be current and certain of himself at every hour of the day and night; I cannot rely on myself ("I make mistakes.")

An additional factor may have been decisive: His striking perception of the simple and necessary element of the present subject had one deficiency. It was a truth that did not figure on the blind passion and dullness of the masses. Whether they be the educated, the officers, or the workers, these masses possess the actual power in all acute situations, where democratically everything turns on the next elections and the response of current public opinion. Max Weber saw all this clearly, but he saw it as he saw scientific truths. Precisely here he remained aloof from what he recognized as correct and in his sovereign insight he not only lacked the naïveté, instinctive shrewdness, and indifference of the politician, but also the effectiveness of the rare, popular leader who, existing in the actual forces of life, not only sees them but absorbs them into his soul itself as motivating forces.

The proposal of the German leaders' voluntary surrender, proper in a heroic world, is understandable; he forgot for a moment that such things are hardly still possible in the contemporary world. It can also be understood that he forthwith publicly spoke with contempt for the revolution; the consequence was that the government rejected Max

Weber when his name was suggested for a leading office. The republican government, like the monarchical government before it, could not use him. He again understood this situation. In his work *Politics as a Vocation* he developed those politician's qualities even he possessed: passion, responsibility, and proportion. Then, however, he perceived how external veracity does not mix with political action, that there is an ethos the politician follows from responsibility for the actual consequences of his mundane actions. Passion for truth, and hatred for the petty and the ordinary always stood in his way. When thinking clearly he probably knew how it could be done, but his ethical sentiments destroyed his tolerance for lying, deceit, and illusions—the veil over reality that the masses need. He was right in a much deeper sense, notwithstanding his nervous disorders, when he said: "I make mistakes."

Max Weber's Lost Possibility of Leadership

Many people nevertheless asked: What would have happened if Max Weber had led Germany? People answered: He would only have caused political disaster; he was too self-willed, no one could work with him unless he obeyed him, he was inflexible in situations; though amiable, his self-righteousness suppressed others, and at one time or another, he always said too much. All these judgments are false.

Max Weber's qualities could only be viewed in such a manner by those who did not love him because they, as rational beings only, did not dare to engage their consciences in a struggle with him. They would then have learned how his passionate temperament, at the same time inflamed and restrained, made possible communication through which people meet and come to mutual understanding, trust, and agreement.

Concerning the disaster: With Max Weber's leadership, a true politics would have been possible whereby the German nation would again constantly face the situation: See what is necessary in rising, see what is true, dare to act without self-deception; or, annihilate Max Weber in its urge for veiling reality. Before the war, if Max Weber had had his way, the bourgeoisie and the workers would have fought the system for the sake of genuine leadership of the state, and limited the monarchy in favor of parliamentary power, at the risk of being sent to jail for such precipitous actions. Max Weber's illness at this time removed this possibility. During the war he would have required a voluntary decision from the people for the sake of veracity. Probably, with each attempt to lead earnestly, Max Weber would quickly have been shoved aside. If they followed him, however, with fate so against us, as it was even without Max Weber, Germany would have viewed the figure of a heroic will and an unforgettable claim at its helm. How different from than when it only staggered under the emperor to preserve the heroic and the moral in the anonymity of the army and the people.

The period of revolution showed Max Weber's capabilities, however. There were events without effect and therefore without historical significance, but for those involved at that time they had a power of symbolic revelation that could be shocking even in the minor features. There are two examples of this:

In a mass meeting attended predominantly by workers, in the days of the workers' and soldiers' councils, Max Weber explained the illusions socialism indulged, the possible and the impossible, and what the actual question was—all uncomfortable truths that mercilessly destroyed the ruling proletariat's fantastic self-delusions. Max Weber no more wanted to flatter the populace than did the previous monarchy. His delivery was so calm, objective, and forcible, and he himself so sustained by the ethos taking hold of him that, after uproarious interruptions, everything finally yielded to the magic of this truthful human being's genuine demagoguery. One could believe that he would be able to carry them along. It was only for a moment, however, for, in the long run the masses are guided by cruder motives than by that which, for a vanishing moment, just once becomes inconceivably clear to them.

When Germany was faced with the peace terms accepted in Versailles, Max Weber explained the situation before a mass meeting of students.[36] World power was lost. Every possible humiliation, including an admission of guilt, was demanded of Germany. This impotence prevented further achievement. Only honor could be saved, and from the seed of heroic defeat perhaps a new future could develop that we will not see any more. Max Weber realized, in the middle of his objective discussions: If we reject the terms and the enemy invades, then you know what to do. We know from the methods of the Russian Revolution of 1905 what even impotence can do. It means abandoning all hope; our fate is the prison and the summary court; but the first Pole who dares to enter Danzig meets a bullet. If you are ready for it, if it comes to that, you will find me; come over to where I am! He accompanied these words, ex-pressed with calm certainty, with a powerful spread-ing motion of his arm. Weber continued: But as long as Germany is down, let us act appropriately; let us no longer show signs of pride of a powerful people when they become merely facade and self-deception;

therefore, no more *couleurs;*[37] whoever still wears *couleurs,* so long as Germany is down, is a cur. No one replied; a silence ensued as if no one had understood. The following day members of student societies marched up and down outside Max Weber's house in protest, wearing their *couleurs.* As an old member of a students' society, Weber returned his ribbon.

Even now, Max Weber remained without a following. It was as though he did not even exist. He did not influence events in the slightest. Never again did he utter a word directing a request for sabotage against the enemy, with defeat a certainty.

He cooperated when the practical work of experts was required, such as in working out the details of the *Reich's* [Weimar] constitution. He is responsible for the constitutionally strong position of the *Reich* president. Historically, it was probably Weber's only extraordinarily effective action. He introduced into the constitution what could become the source for the possibility of a new democratically established authority and real leadership in Germany.

Constitutional work, nevertheless, is something other than political action; it is its genesis. Here Max Weber's profound insight could be completely brought to bear. But political action itself, however, was at an end for him, even before he had actually attempted it. He returned to his scholarly work, as he had so often done, and in 1920 resigned from the German Democratic Party. On the question of socialization this party accommodated Marxism, which seemed impossible for Max Weber: "The politician *must* make compromises—the *scholar must* not cover them."[38] Thus, upon his death in 1920, he was definitely out of all politics and concentrating entirely on science.

The Enduring Claim of Max Weber's Political Thinking

In retrospect, Max Weber is like a vision of the genius of the German people who saw, suffered, advised, and was powerless, far from the helm directed by incompetent hands. What then were disregarded insights are today's truisms. Many people, upon reading his works, would probably like to claim him for their own party purposes or, because he followed no party line, reproach him for an inconsistent political posture. Democrats, nationalists, and socialists seem to get their ammunition here, but each one should ask whether, in his own political thought and action, he satisfies Max Weber's true demands which endure independently of parties, constantly changing situations, and special interests.

Weber's sense of what is proper to political life is seen as the *"fact of power."* Politics is struggle; struggle demands a leader who cannot delegate responsibility, like an official whose honor depends upon conscientiously carrying out the demands of higher authority and law. The political leader bears responsibility himself. Since he operates in the world, however, where power is the specific external means for him, he cannot act according to an absolute moral law without considering the consequences, trusting in God for success. Thus, he would act "principle ethically," but irresponsibly. Since he wants to attain something in the world, he must act and reckon with the powers that operate in it. Whoever engages in politics "must deal . . . with the diabolical forces that lie in wait in every exercise of force."[39] Also, whoever wishes to produce justice on earth needs the human *apparatus of a following.* This does not function without the gratification of hatred and revenge, "resentment and the requirement for a pseudo-ethical dogmatism . . . ,"[40] not without "adventure, victory, spoils, power, and benefices."[41] "The leader is completely dependent on the functioning of this, his apparatus for his success. Therefore, on its motives, not his own. . . . What he actually achieves under such conditions of his acting is therefore not up to him but is prescribed for him by those ethically and predominantly base motives of the actions of his

followers. . . ."[42] "Trained ruthlessness in viewing
the realities of life, the capability of enduring them
and coping with them"[43] makes the true politician.
He does not hold responsible the stupidity and vul-
garity of the world he well knows and surmises—but
himself. He has the "tenacity of heart that has also
coped with the shattering of all hopes . . ."[44] and is
able to say "nevertheless!"[45] in the face of everything.

Others, however, need to sense the necessity of a
statesman who leads. To educate them, Weber
makes the essential difference between a *civil servant*
and a *politician* clear: from the former, impartial
administration without wrath and prejudice and
from the latter, struggle; from the former, the self-
denial of obedience and from the latter, inclusive
self-accountability. "Eminent civil servants with
high moral standards are poor politicians, above all,
irresponsible in the political sense of the term and in
this sense: morally inferior politicians. . . ."[46] That
Germany was governed by civil servants was the
misfortune of the system. It accounts for Weber's ire
against "the thoroughly *petit bourgeois* hostility of
the leaders of all parties . . . ,"[47] but all the more so
against the false leaders, the braggarts with their
declamations, against "the narrow-minded and vain
upstarts of the moment," who only ask about their
own individual function, but serve no cause.

Something else must be demanded for sensing the fact of power, so that something substantial may operate in the will for power. "Even the flight to creatural futility weighs on the externally strongest political successes"[48] if there is no *belief*. For Weber, this belief in politics is realized in the will to serve the external goals of everyday life, but in the notion of people, not merely of the well-being, but of the nobility of our nature. This belief can only be effective if the fact of power sets limits for itself in the will of the people themselves.

Therefore, a cheap way out would have the sense for political essence subside into an enthusiasm for indeterminate power in general and for the nation as a mere fact. Inner *veracity* is rather as much a condition of permanent political success as of the nobility of those ascending to it. For that reason, Weber has always turned against illusions: propaganda and false promises in war, as at the time of the revolution; the spurious belief in mere wishing; the camouflaging of facts; the misuse of nationalism for promoting class interests; the safeguarding of political stupidity; the covering up of internal political struggles; the "degradation of the fatherland's name to a demagogic party label"; the attitude in political arguments that shamelessly directly contradicts yesterday's statements today (e.g. in 1916, after the opening of submarine warfare: "Fourteen days ago, they said 'The

Americans will never attack'—they now say: 'The Americans want a war in any case—quite like Italy at the time.)"[49] He therefore finally turned against mock justice in favor of the simple guarantee of law. When Count Arco[50] was pardoned after murdering Eisner, Max Weber told the students:

> You extolled Count Arco because he behaved chivalrously in court and [was] manly in every respect, as is also my conviction. His deed resulted from the conviction that Kurt Eisner brought shame after shame upon Germany. I also have this opinion.
> Nevertheless, it is a grave weakness to pardon him as long as the law prevails, and if I had been minister, I would have had him shot. . . . Political murders will set a precedent.[51]

An eye for the fact of power, belief bearing responsibility and veracity are prerequisites for political thinking, but they all require *expertise*. The trained official, as a specialist, faces the dilettante; so too does the statesman as a genuine leader, essentially different from the specialized official, face the vain demagogue. The statesman's knowledge is not specific in the wrong sense, but besides his innate calling, he also needs practice in self-education for detaching himself from things and from himself, therewith, for the "ability of letting realities make an

impression on him with inner composure and serenity. . . ."[52] Vanity, the mortal enemy of all objective
devotion, is the source of incompetence and irresponsibility because it drives one to be in the fore-
front as visibly as possible. Political expertise can be
acquired only by constantly conquering the vanity
common to all people, which is less detrimental in
all other areas. Emotional politics, the politics of
hatred, only causes trouble because of its lack of
objectivity; even the tone of its political speeches
may miss their potential political effect. Weber was
thus infuriated over the decades, be it by the clamor
about the colonies, the wording of speeches and
notes during the war, the boasting talk of power, the
saber-rattling, or the confessions of guilt and ethical
dogmatism. Only with such self-education in political thinking can expertise secure concrete knowledge
that is, at times, needed and infinitely diversified.

Weber demanded and himself embodied a genuine *belief in his own people, without illusions* and an
ability to tell the truth even when it is reluctantly
heard, whenever this truth is politically relevant.
This truth is abysmally separated from the demagogic fanaticism of truth, which insincerely states
what is pleasing, tramples the powerless, or represents a challenging, insulting design or the mere
discharge of hatred. Max Weber evolved German

political thinking, not national gossip. His real success endured in all the tensions of his political consciousness: The rise of the Germans, the last criterion meant truly and in concrete certainty. "For the re-establishment of Germany in its old glory, I would certainly align myself with any power on earth and even with the devil incarnate, but not with the power of stupidity."[53]

The uncanny boundary where the conscious responsibility ethic seems to call the principle ethic into question, though finally the former exists only through the latter, shows contrasting pairs as ethical paradoxes. With their elucidation, Weber puts the onus on everyone who naïvely supposes the only correct answer to be mere rational justice.

What the ultimate goal may be, however, is lost in indetermination: The dignity of the person and the political worth of the nation throughout the world—not one without the other—to him meant the wish that people in the future would recognize us as their ancestors, not necessarily in the sense of race and lineage, but in the manner that we know the Greeks, to whom we owe our existence.

Max Weber as a Scientist

Max Weber's mastery of enormous fields of knowledge, his familiarity with the most diverse sciences, his understanding of the methods of natural science and humanities, his professional training in law, his grasp of theology, his facility in the history of millennia, in China and India, the East and West—this would merely signify the rare mental capacity of his mind. His research acquired its axis, however, only by the fact that everything was related to people and, more specifically, to people in a historically changing society. Whether Weber was investigating the psychophysics of industrial labor, pursuing the rational connections of theological dogmas, or comparatively investigating the significance of the patterns of the city in all cultures, the question was always how people, determined by recognizable dependencies, bring forth in action a meaning they did not at all intend. Instead of devoting himself to the hopeless attempt to bring one basic meaning of all that happens to a truly valid insight, or to finding the governing law of all things or the entirety of being, he took up the ascertainable meaning, intended by real people and produced in its dependencies and consequences that are only, at times, relatively perceptible in sporadic contexts. His research, therefore, is apparently dispersed into infinity, although related to a single idea whose fulfillment remains an unending task. His research, therefore, cannot even be adequately demonstrated by portraying the findings or rendering the entire picture, but can only be made tangible in its direction.

Examples of Weberian Insights

First of all, a view of Max Weber's special method of insights, acquired from the connections of human things, can be gained by two examples:

1. The *decline of the ancient world* has been a subject of amazement and inquiry since Montesquieu and Gibbon. Max Weber saw the demonstrable error of speaking about moral decay and racial degeneration as the cause of the decline. One com-

pletely singular factor is convincingly stated against it by him. Towards the end of the Roman Republic, ancient culture was capitalistically based on a plantation economy with slaves that were constantly being newly bought. Previously, the slaves were held in a patriarchal manner; they had families and propagated. Now they were dealt with capitalistically. Kept in barracks, they were driven to work in chains by overseers. Since there was now a steady need for replacement slaves, this form of economy lasted down to the wars of Trajan,[54] as long as great wars brought new slaves to market. With the pacification of the empire, however, the supply of slaves ceased and a shortage occurred; this form of economy had to be abandoned. The slaves were allowed families again in order to propagate. From barracks inmates they became colonies, bound to the soil, and again participated in their existence with a special interest. They became living people in a natural economical way. The superstructure of the capitalistic economy thus became narrower and narrower, but since it had ultimately sustained the Roman state, the army, and the economic trade of the Mediterranean region that had become the *orbis terrarum,* the return to a natural economy signified, economically, the transition to the Middle Ages, with relations interlacing all countries breaking off. Militarily, the Roman mili-

tary organization, which was based on wages, dissolved; politically, the unity of the empire was unten-
able. The increasing defenselessness of the Roman
Empire had, therefore, originated in the third century.

Herewith, Max Weber did not quite grasp perhaps the decline of the ancient world, but only
brought to light *one* demonstrable cause.

2. Another example directly brings up the final
comprehensive question for Weber. The *spirit of
capitalistic economic leadership* that sustains our
present-day existence has not really existed anywhere
else in history in its present form. There was indeed
reckless greed and hunger for gold; there were even
repeated capitalistic enterprises in which great profits were attained by investing large monetary posses-
sions. But nowhere was there anything like today:
Most of the needs of the masses are satisfied through
an accurate, numerically exact calculation of an-
ticipated costs and profits, with an incomparably
developed technology, in an organization of indus-
tries that exist permanently independent of individuals.

For this to become possible, several assumptions
were required: first, the actual computation of all
costs even to the wage limit in work contracts (contrasted to the incalculability of the costs of slave

labor); second, the rational prediction of expected legal decisions, only possible under the recognition of a formal jurisprudence, not with the administration of an irrational justice unpredictably dependent upon the good will of a judge; third, a state order in which the rational, knowable law governs, not a party or despot, and with no arbitrary action at all. The formal jurisprudence, legal state order, and the disappearance of slavery are conditions that commonly rationalize existence for the benefit of calculability.

But all these conditions would not have sufficed *to produce* the spirit of an effective capitalistic disposition of work. For this, Weber finds rather another originally decisive factor: The disposition of the worker who prefers work for an impersonal industry over personal service, performing, in return for remuneration, work regulated by contract; who untiringly promotes at work the thing set for him and is in other respects free; who has an inner relationship with the disposition of the employer who wears himself out building up his plant, reinvesting his profits for the expansion and strengthening of his operation, who serves his undertaking but never really gets to enjoy his profits. Viewed from the standpoint of vivacious enjoyment, both actually work to no purpose; both have an occupational idea. Today this spirit becomes apparent mostly in over-specialized humanity and in empty, always exhausting, calculating struggles for success, yet with the moral recognition of the occupational idea. The question is: Whence does this spiritual impulse come, which did not exist, as a rule, anywhere in the world? It has a religious source that has since disappeared, that today in the occupational way of thinking has become purely worldly. The occupational idea has its source in Luther; its specific development, which first had those remarkable consequences, in Calvinism. The religious doctrine was: A human being should not serve God like a monk in an asceticism that pushes him out of the world into loveless inactivity; rather God wants to be glorified *in* the world by asceticism. Consequently, a human being should work for others so that God's will may be done in the world through successful works; he should not work for pleasure in profits and success; rather, he should not take pleasure in them. He should produce in an intrinsically worldly asceticism, with only the following gained in the process: God has predestined all people either for the eternal state of grace or for eternal damnation; no human being can change this, but he can search for indications as to which state he has been determined by God's inexplicable decree. He can never know it for certain; it always remains questionable. One indication is his success in the world, as determined by his actions—the untiring planning and producing of the employer and worker—not as a matter of gain or worldly pleasure but as a sign of his destination for the state of grace. If he were to enjoy his gain instead of using it for the further expansion of his success and, therefore, the glorification of God in the world, this would become a sign of the contrary. The doubtfulness of the state of grace that still remains, even with the grandest indications of success, drives him restlessly on. This religious conception, assimilated into the disposition of many people, became a unique impulse of labor otherwise calculated along rational lines. Economic leadership at once worldly and ascetic arose from it; the purely worldly form endures spectrally today with the asceticism now rendered meaningless in combination with new motives.

More complicated and more convincing than this schematic abstract is the analysis of Max Weber's most complete scientific work, regarding the connections between the Protestant ethic and the spirit of capitalism. But if we ask whether Max Weber believed that he had understood the cause of modern capitalism, he answers: By no means. With all the means of empirical research and comprehending interpretation, he merely sets forth the conditions and then a positive factor that invisibly achieved results no one before had understood. These investigations expand the consciousness by enlightening a concealed connection that could only operate because it was concealed; and they assist us in comprehending the remaining shell whenever the substance of the source has vanished.

Max Weber's interests are universally aimed at *that which is characteristic of the West* and at the question of why that became so here and not anywhere else. The mode of rational science (the Greeks), the liberation from magic (the Jews), the civil autonomy of cities, the types of professional politicians and demagogues, the constitutional state, the rational bureaucratic state, technical development, and so on are objects of inquiry formulated in economic terms as the basic question, which was also the impetus for the investigation of the Protestant ethic: *Why do we have capitalism in the West?* Why only here, while the possibilities also existed almost everywhere else? A characteristic feature of capitalism is rationalism: exact calculation, reckoning in general. Indeed, there was rationalism everywhere in the world, but ours was unlimited. The broader, more comprehensive question is therefore that of the *source* and *consequences* of the *rationalization* of the human spirit. To answer these questions, universal history, as it appears to Max Weber, unfolds.

The Universal Historian

The scientist Max Weber wanted to know what is, because that which was known *concerned* him. Living primarily in the present, he wanted to *know* as a politician or a potential politician. Thus, he asked politically: How does it happen that the leadership of the German state is directing us downhill? What do we really want politically? But the nation was only *one* point of departure for Max Weber's sociological will for knowledge. It was a question of our *state of the world in general.* To understand this requires a universal history; and to understand any historical event conversely again requires delving into our own present world. Just by concentrating on the present as his own historical existence does Max Weber become a universal historian. The impotence of his political will transformed his strength into an accelerated, passionate will for knowledge. His awakening consciousness brought him a unique knowledge of all times and cultures and came to the aid of his historical interest.

In his universal history, he did not seek the grand *images* of past times and cultures nor the stage of world history. Everything imageful was merely a means to him. Although he portrayed unheard of power, portraits played a slight role in all his works.

Whoever goes to them expecting to find easily comprehensible stories, descriptions, and well-rounded figures will be disappointed. He will hardly find his way through the maze of what was mentioned and touched on. Weber presupposes in his reader a knowledge and view of history, but measured by the penetration and objective certainty of this historical understanding, most portrayals by historical writers sink into the imprecise, the floating, the atmospheric.

As a universal historian, Max Weber also did not seek the whole human world. He knew that its existence was questionable, endless, and for research, inexhaustible. Because he was looking for the tangible facts of an event, he was acquainted with only relative entireties and did not look for the dominating *construction of the whole* of human affairs. Measured by Weber's universal history, the richest historical-philosophical entirety works poorly, even though seductively, through easy-going grandeur.

With these renunciations, Max Weber did not become a collector of historical facts. He did not seek an *encyclopedic survey* of everything of which we have knowledge. Measured by the tersely reflective multiplicity of Weberian perspectives, such an encyclopedia functions diffusely.

He also could not be enticed to persistently gaze

upon figures and directly observe dependencies. He did not seek *formative* satisfaction as the ultimate goal in representing the *intellectual order* of *human reality*. Measured by the reference to Weberian insights on the binding force of human existence determining itself in the world, this formation acts like a blessed, non-binding gratification of greatness in passively courageous, skeptical despair.

Therefore, Max Weber, the universal historian, is neither a portrayer like *Ranke*, [55] nor a philosopher of history like *Hegel*, nor a collector of data like *Schmoller*, [56] nor a contemplator of figures like *Burckhardt*, [57] but a sociologist. Portrayal, construction, collection, and exposition serve him as means of limited importance. While he does not allow himself to be entrapped by any of these as an aim, the world of human events is completely opened to his inquiry into their causes. His sociology is universal history through incomplete ascent to the *radical questions* in order to arrive, comprehending, at the great *decisions*, the last *origins* in the transformation of human events. He wished to understand how human existence came into being, from determinable factors. He wished to know and at the same time clarify the limits of knowledge. Despite his knowledge, which probably seemed to others a complete penetration of things, he, therefore, had an unceasing dread of the real which is never recognized as such—but only in certain respects.

The Method (Possibility, Comparison, Ideal Type)

As history becomes for Max Weber a means of finding the consciousness and intention of present reality, he thus sought the view of the past as contemporary. Essentially, his *consciousness of the present* was that he did not yet consider it as already history and necessarily happening in a certain way—the person considering it in this manner is not at all living in the present, but is an imaginary spectator of something that is always in the past. But for him his *consciousness of the past* became another present and thereby became actually real—whoever considers the historical as mere past, involuntarily and incorrectly makes it similar to his own present. Only in this way could Weber bring to the greatest clarity, historically and currently, what really happened.

He himself articulated the method essential to this process: We must see the possibilities in order to grasp what is real. In the present, a sketch of what is possible is the sphere in which I become certain of what I decide; without possibility, I have no freedom; without seeing the possible, I act blindly; only with the knowledge of the possible do I know what I am actually doing. Analogous to that is the category of "objective possibility" in the historical conception of past situations. The historian imagines a situation. The extent of his knowledge permits him to construct what was possible at that time. With these constructions, he first measures as possible what was *known* to the persons acting decisively at that time. Then he measures by the possible what really *happened* in order to ask what the *specific* cause was of this real result that came to be out of several possible results. The historian once again transforms into possibility what has already actually happened in order to find the critical point of the decision by which it happened. Referring to the logical works of others, Max Weber called the cause found for the actual event the adequate cause. In other words: What happened is also not understood as absolutely necessary, following strict laws. Rather, according to our knowledge of principles, we can understand that it happened in such a way because, if we ourselves were involved, we would expect such an occurrence.

One way of finding the possible is *comparison.* As a universal historian, Max Weber constantly relates quite unusual events to each other. He compares developments in China, India, and the West not to find historical laws or sociological types as abstractions of the identical or the similar. Rather, the coinciding element is the means used to arrive at a more resolute understanding of that which is actually different. In similar historical situations, something similar is possible. Hence, in the course of time, the opposite or simply something different occurs. By comparison and contrast the source of each particular can be found which, for its part, is conceived as possibility. In this way, Max Weber arrived at the clearest knowledge of what happened at any given time. He necessarily got there only on the path of universal history. There is a correlation between universal history and the resolute understanding of concrete connections. In Max Weber's sociological analyses, therefore, the element of this form that is found throughout is: Exaggerating through comparisons and limitations of the possible what was determinant in any sense for the continuation of the events. Whether he deals with the origin of the Jewish prophecy, the significance of Jewry for world history, the lack of progress in India, or the significance of the battles of Marathon and Salamis, it is the cardinal point throughout that is brought into the field of view with the breadth of versatile empirical research by reason of which only the finally simple element also becomes apparent.

In order to compare human matters, I must interpret the facts through concepts that denote their meaning—either as the intended meaning of those acting, the possible meaning through its significance for other things, or as an objective meaning in the sense of accuracy. Reality is an infinite weaving of the meaningful and the meaningless. In order to seize it, constructed concepts are necessary which, developed in themselves as meaningfully consistent, serve only as standards for reality, to see how far it conforms to those concepts. Weber calls these constructed concepts *ideal types.* To him, they are the perceptive-technical means of approaching reality, not reality itself. They are not generic concepts under which the real is suggested, but meaningful concepts by which reality is measured, in so far as it corresponds to them, in order to precisely comprehend it and to bring out clearly as a fact the element that does not conform to them. They are not the aim of knowledge, not the laws of what has happened, but a means to gain the clearest awareness of the specific characteristics of human reality at the present time. The wealth of Weberian insights rests on the construction of such ideal types, demonstrated as fruitful for the concrete knowledge of the real; e.g. the types of authority, such as traditional, charismatic, bureaucratic; the types of churches and sects; the types of cities; and so on. The ideal typical concepts are to be sharply developed; there are discontinuities among them. Reality, however, is fluid; in it everything seems to become blurred in transitions.

The Distinctions

It is an inextinguishable impulse of the uncritical will for knowledge to grasp truth recognizable as generally valid, as the one whole and definite element, so that by it I know what is good, what I should do, and what reality itself is. Max Weber's critical discerning opposes this monistic impulse. He cogently desired valid knowledge gained through experience, and as a scientist, persevered in distinctions to retain those he advanced in the service of genuine knowledge as well as genuine philosophizing. He, therefore, struggled for the real achievement of the distinctions: between *knowledge gained through experience* and *value judgment;* between a *particular knowledge* that is always *one-sided* and all modes of *grasping totality;* between *empirical reality* and the *essence of being.*

1. Max Weber has inexorably repeated: No *empirical research* can establish what has value and what I *should do.* Knowledge gained through experience, with an assumed purpose, can indeed indicate the means that serve its advancement or detract from it,

and the secondary results of an action by which other values are impaired. But it can never demonstrate the value and the purpose themselves as generally binding. On the contrary, the clarity of knowledge gained through experience, as well as that of resolute valuing and choosing, rests on the neat distinction of both. The value freedom of science means reserving its own judgments in order to clearly see the facts of a case from all sides, prior to seeing the desired, and even the uncomfortable facts. The scientific obligation to see the truth of the facts and the practical obligation to stand up for one's own ideals are different. This does not mean that the fulfillment of the one is not possible without the fulfillment of the other. Weber only opposes their mixture; only their separation permits pure realization of both. Scientific objectivity and lack of principle have no relationship. Their mixture, however, destroys both objectivity and principle. Max Weber rejects the process to speak apparently objectively, supposedly to derive a generally valid value judgment from the matter as a half-measure that cannot permit value judgments on the one hand, and that strives to reject the responsibility for its judgments on the other. Only distance from the object and from itself enables calm questioning of what is real and possible. But resolute valuations that are held back in perception are, in turn, themselves essential conditions of knowledge because they sensitively educate for every possible valuation.

According to Weber, the value freedom of science then does not mean that valuations should not be made in life, but just the reverse: The passion of valuing and willing first of all produces the genuine objectivity of research ability as its own illumination and self-education. Value freedom furthermore does not mean that valuations, whether actually carried out and possible, should not be a subject of research; rather, they are the essential subject for the investigation of human matters. Through value freedom alone arises that distance in the investigation of every valuation, of its meaning, its source, and its consequences that really brings it to consciousness and makes it evident. Finally, value freedom does not mean to him that the choice of problems approaching investigation does not rest on valuations; rather, a value judgment that concerns me is the supposition of genuine passion in research.

2. Max Weber recognized that all research is *particular* and that the *whole* is closed. If I were able to know what is general in human matters, be it general, unalterably similar natural law, be it a totality, be it an unequivocal principle of development, I could derive the particular event from them as necessary. However, I recognize among relative viewpoints rules and laws that touch mere aspects of

what is real, and I recognize only relative entireties, never the whole. Reality is individual, infinite, inexhaustible in every form; the laws that are valid for it cannot be used to derive what is real. There is also no general, temporal, primordial state, cosmic or human, from which historical individuation may develop as it could from a general state untroubled by historical contingency. Reality is always equally individual in historical, infinite multiplicity. Thus, there is no generalization, either conceptually or temporally; there is no principle, no substance, no human original situation or original essence, no existence that has yet been individually undetermined, from which can be derived what is real. This was Max Weber's horizon when he said: "The stream of immeasurable happening rolls endlessly toward eternity."[58] Therefore, man can only penetrate reality through experimental science, not deduce it and apprehend it as entirety. The result of this insight is, on the one hand, the *resolute comprehension of empirical reality* and on the other the *rejection of all metaphysical encroachments* on knowledge gained through experience.

What is empirically real must be definitely demonstrable. In human action it is only the meaning *intended* by people (as distinguished from an imputed, objective, historical meaning unknown by those acting); it is, further, the meaning intended by the *individual* and many individuals (whereas entire human groups that act unconsciously as such are not empirically ascertainable); only the action of individuals is empirically real. Producing conceptions of entireties is not the concern of empirical sociology; it investigates these as effective conceptions, inherent in people, according to their functional significance; neither does it absolutize them, nor does it deny their reality established differently and not generally valid, nor does it decide that they must not be used in action. Its individualistic method does not mean individualistic valuation, any more than the rationalistic character of its formation of concepts signifies belief in the predominance of rational motives in human action. Empirical research inevitably dissolves the substantial concepts of state, church, marriage, and so on in themselves without touching them as forms of belief; rather, it investigates them again as such, in their objectivity as concepts believed by people and as effective motive for them. For sociology itself, therefore, the substance believed is transformed into the object of rational knowledge as meaningful content, willed and intended by real people: the state is "solely a *possibility* that one action laid upon another in a specifiable way, according to its content of meaning, took place, or takes place, or will take place. . . . Another *clear* meaning cannot be connected to the statement that . . . a 'state' still . . . 'exists'. . ."[59]

Therefore, Max Weber, as an *empirical sociologist,* is opposed to metaphysical concepts such as the spirit of the people, and the idea as an existing force against the concept of necessary development and the materialistic conception of history as an unequivocal determination of the course of world history. No vision of the whole of human history, no construction of world history is permissible to him. He continues an immensely methodical penetration through empirical research. No rounded whole is formed. If he had a system, it could only be a system of temporary methods and basic concepts. But even this closed system of concepts is not a meaningful aim. "The points of departure in the cultural sciences thereby remain variable into the limitless future as long as a Chinese torpidity of intellectual life does not break humanity's habit of asking new questions of life that always remain unalterably inexhaustible."[60]

The relativity of all concepts suitable for the knowledge of empirical reality unites the breadth of possibilities of knowledge with temporary one-sidedness; the precision of what was meant at times unites perspicuity with abstractness. The presumed knowledge of totality as the entire development of world history, the true reality upon which everything else depends, are taken up by Weber, but only as ideal typical constructions possible and questioned for their fecundity of concrete knowledge of realities. Thus, he took up the Marxist constructions, rejecting their absoluting and ideological totalizing; he thus attempted, on the same plane, to show the originality of religious factors, in their limited effectiveness, for the history of economics and society, and to articulate to what extent, with empirical investigation, that which appeared to others as only dependent superstructure could have primary causal significance.

By examining all concepts and constructions according to the criterion of the extent to which they pose questions leading to essential results in empirical research, Weber made possible the acquisition of all accessible viewpoints for every reality. Just because he did not admit any kind of completion of knowledge, let no total view pass scientifically, or recognized no knowledge of the "proper" factors of what has occurred, he acquired the boundless perspectives and orientations which are the essence of impartial knowledge. To him, indeed, no human world could be entirely explained but, rather, is an infinite problem. Through it he definitely has reliable knowledge and was able to avoid widespread delusions by viewing the whole, the forces, and by not absolutizing one-sided views. In entering into radically one-sided conceptions representing all knowledge, he overcame their domination through knowledge of their one-sidedness while, conversely, he dominated them.

3. Because Max Weber, as an empirical scientist, preferred particular knowledge to entireties, the particular to the general, concrete research to theoretical reflection, penetrating discernment to surveys and labels, causal analysis to imagery, intellectual construction to mere description, the solution into empirically tangible factors to substantial entities, he remained *distanced from the core of things* while grasping *empirical reality* (in another context, this purity of the knowable world becomes the condition of love for the actual being). His extraordinary proximity to reality did not mean knowledge of essences. Max Weber by no means believed that he had grasped reality itself in its ultimate cause. In the context in which he most thoroughly examined the empirical material, he expounded a causal factor about the dependence of modern capitalism on the Protestant ethic, but said firmly: The fact that *one* causal factor is present is evident; whether its quantative significance is great or small is not evident. I consider it great. Since being cannot directly become a subject of empirical research, Weber grasps *every* mode of empirical existence, losing himself in none,

examining each for its causal significance. The natural conditions, technical means, situational connections as ideas and purposes intended by people, religious conceptions in their consequences, as well as the fact of power of political connections, all became for him empirical subjects of relative significance. In the process Max Weber, in his empirical investigating, runs all the more resolutely into sources, as not fully comprehended assumptions, as his point of departure.

The Science of Sociology

Max Weber's investigations are the purest effect of modern realistic perception—attaining certain clearness only in the natural sciences and mathematics—on the whole of human existence. He called this investigation sociology, and he thereby included it with the efforts bearing this name although he owed no more to these sociological efforts than to the historical sciences, the philosophy of history, and jurisprudence. Sociology as an empirical science, however, was not allowed to reach into boundless areas; he limited it to the level of interpretation meant in human action in so far as this action was related to the behavior of others. How he tilled this field with his unheard of knowledge cannot be conveyed in a brief description; the most concrete of his individual investigations serves the endless progress of universal insight into what people have done and what is possible for them.

Officially, Max Weber was a political economist. He opposed the establishment of professorial chairs in sociology, not concealing the fact that sociology deals with a science that treads on the feet of other sciences, requiring considerable individual research experience in these other individual sciences and an extraordinary measure of criticism. "Most of what goes by the name sociology is a fraud," he said in his Heidelberg valedictory address.

Non-knowledge in Knowledge

Max Weber's science is double-edged. We do not understand the one if we forget the other.

Universal empiricism desires to know what is knowable in general. It steps in when something can be demonstrated. For it, everything takes place according to intelligible causal laws and rational conclusive connections. Everything?

Only that which is knowable, and everything in so far as everything and the knowable are identical. Nothing can occur to possible knowledge, except what falls to its relativizing. But knowledge pushes against *limits.* Max Weber's science is linked with the awareness of what is not known. First of all, the infinity of everything that is individual is indeed inexhaustible. Then this infinity, as historical uniqueness, has, under certain circumstances, a significance whose interpretation cannot fully be achieved. Finally, the source is always somehow assumed: The first conceptions of a religion cannot be genetically understood despite all identification of constellations and situations without which they would not have originated.

There is cause for *misunderstandings* with this duality of knowledge and non-knowledge by which empirical knowledge seems to prevail almost exclusively as the "disenchantment of the world" in Max Weber's works. This enormous knowledge transposed into research is incorrectly interpreted as knowledge of human existence *in itself;* some are foolishly satisfied with it or reject it.

He has, thus, perhaps been criticized for having no sense of religion, Indian philosophy, the world of farmers and real estate owners, the integrity and substantiality of the state, and so on. All these reproaches, however, are based on a confusion of generally valid knowledge *of* something with the being *in* something expressing itself by reflecting on a meaning. Every source as known is no longer itself, but rather in the form of a relative—knowing what is *meant*. Max Weber purified knowledge as empirical knowledge, but not in order to limit thinking to empirical knowledge; rather, in order to make clearly and decidedly possible other ways of thinking with their different meanings and value bases, always historical but not generally valid. His veracity forbade him to make compromises regarding those representing their own interests by not wishing to know the facts, proclaiming their cause as a knowable general interest; he made no compromises with the negativism of the yearning unbelievers who, in knowledge, try to take as possession what they have lost in belief. It is characteristic that true believers take no offense at Max Weber's religious-sociological analyses, that those genuinely rooted in the political fact of power of the state have no objection to his cool, empirical statements. To grasp the knowable in its relativeness throws belief all the more purely into bold relief.

Another criticism is as follows: Knowledge in the form of Weberian research has grown out of control, for people could no longer master this enormous mass of material. Knowledge becomes meaningless because it serves no purpose, scattered as it is into infinity without substance. Thus, this accomplishment of Max Weber may be his last and his path may now be at an end. However, this reproach confuses the infinity of empty intellectuality with the infinity of the substantial research process.

Finally, the critics claimed that Max Weber floundered as a scientist. He did, in fact, flounder, but in the sense of the true floundering that is inherent in the meaning of real science. Fictitious is the floundering in the intellectuality of arbitrary thoughts and distinct schemas which, for a time, apparently satisfy intellectually but then leave one behind in a void of meaninglessness. Fictitious is the floundering that, just because it does not master infinity, resignedly abandons the path of the possibility of knowledge. Fictitious is a floundering that disillusionedly forsakes knowledge in general, because we have incorrectly wished to grasp being, itself, in knowledge. Fictitious floundering pretends not to know and no longer strives. Max Weber's floundering was seizing positively true non-knowledge in the boundless, definite empirical knowledge approaching objectivity and the material, and opening up the possibility of being as true being, not as a known being. As knowledge becomes comprehensive, floundering leads all the more deeply to being; for that reason, Max Weber's research projects were so gigantic that he could never complete them, and his works, despite their scope, are powerful fragments, incomplete buildings of a Titan. The fact that in sociology Max Weber rejected metaphysics even in every disguised form, that he made the scientific way of thinking ascetic, meant that he kept open the possibility of true floundering and impeded the fictitious satisfaction in a science that falsifies itself. Whatever succeeds only when it is genuinely believed should not be facilitated by supposed knowledge. The relativity of knowledge seems to result in a fall into a chasm, but only directly from this fall does the bottom become conscious in the genuine source from the historical present of willing and believing this bottom only becomes pure whenever it is consolidated into veracity and rationality in the fire of a boundless will for knowledge. The broadest horizon brings the particular root to free development.

Max Weber's science, surpassing the development of human strengths, was not an end in itself. It was the function of an existence that it served. Sociology is only an extension of his deeper being which he kept hidden and which only indirectly becomes visible in Max Weber as a philosopher.

Max Weber
as a Philosopher

M ax Weber sketched no philosophical system. It
would be impossible to represent his philosophy as a
doctrine. He refused to be called a philosopher. To
us, however, he is the true philosopher of the time
in which he lived. Because philosophy is not a progressive science that recognizes a timeless truth, it
must at times become reality as historical existence,
coming to pass from the unconditional with a view
towards the transcendent. Max Weber taught no
philosophy; he was a philosophy.

The Expressed Philosophical Positions

Max Weber only peripherally gave to his investigations explicit philosophical discussions on the basis
of his critical conscience, which did not tolerate as
groundless the occurrence of these investigations on

the *meaning of science,* on *possible ultimate view-points,* and on *what he did not intend in his investigations.*

For him, science became the compelling, empirical, and logical insight which, in infinite progressing, is never completed. He stated it: The scientist works in order to be surpassed; he can well have the satisfaction of recognizing something that is certain and definitive; however, that is an isolated element in the endless stream of the perceptible. Science can never perceive the essence of being; it can rather only investigate facts and their connections in its unconcluding progression. It can never say what we should simply do; rather, only indicate the means for its realization in the case of assumed purpose. If science was once considered the way to true being, to true art, to true nature, to true God, and to true happiness, no one believes that any longer. Science has disenchanted everything. It always assumes that something may be important from another source. Medicine, for example, pragmatically maintains that human life has to be unconditionally preserved and suffering reduced; astronomy theoretically maintains that the laws of cosmic occurrences are worth knowing. The fact that science may have meaning can never be demonstrated from itself by itself.

With this Max Weber drew the inexorable inference from science's actual progress. He recalls Plato's attitude by quoting a parable (at the beginning of the seventh book of *The Republic*): People in this life are chained in a cave with a view of the rocks and only see shadows of being that fall on the wall; but when one frees himself, he can turn and see the sun. "He is a philosopher, but the sun is the truth of science which alone does not snatch at illusions and shadows, but at true being."[61] No remnant of this attitude remains today; science does not grant that which Plato believed.

Therefore, Tolstoy concluded, science is meaningless: "It is meaningless, because it gives no answer to the only question important for us: What should we do? How should we live?" Furthermore, because death becomes meaningless through science, death might not *be,* since science is inconcludable and life, which is resigned to death, might have no end, according to its subjective meaning.

Max Weber, contrary to Plato,—at least against the interpretation of his philosophy as a science— declares that it is simply indisputable that science has no answer to Tolstoyian questions of meaning and, contrary to Tolstoy, does not deny the meaning of science. Following neither Plato nor Tolstoy he answers the question of the meaning of science thusly: The generally valid knowledge of the empirically real and logically compelling is something irreplaceable for the man of integrity and independence—the devotion to a cause that is acknowledged without self-interest. Science teaches us to see uncomfortable facts; man proves himself true by experiencing what he can persevere in knowing. Science gives *clarity*. It points out given facts on which my actions depend and makes me conscious of the rational *viewpoint* from which action accordingly follows. It is true in the sense of its own, generally valid, compelling truth only if it is free from prophecy. We can believe or disbelieve the prophets; scientific insight is compelling for everyone, or it is not compelling at all.

The most stimulating of scientific possibilities is the question of ultimate viewpoints. In the *rational clarification of viewpoints*, from which my action or the action of another accordingly follows, Max Weber proceeds

> from the one fundamental fact: That so long as life is based in itself and is comprehended from itself, it knows only the external struggle of those gods with each other—literally stated: The incongruity and thus the inconclusiveness of the struggle for the ultimate, in general, *possible* viewpoints for living necessitates *deciding* among them.[62]
>   . . . as Hellenic man once sacrificed to Aphrodite, and then to Apollo and, above all, as everyone sac-

rificed to the gods of his city, thus it is still today
only that behaviour has been disenchanted and un-
clothed of its mythical but inner true plasticity.
Fate, but quite certainly not 'science' rules over
those gods and their struggles.[63]

To bring to clarity the ultimate viewpoints which
bring this inconcludable conflict into the world,
thereby tragically implicating all human action so
that man can account for the ultimate meaning of
his own action, is the task of science; but which
science? "The specialized discipline of philosophy
and the philosophical principled discussions of the
individual disciplines, according to their essence, attempt to accomplish this."[64]

But it would be a misunderstanding to ascribe to
Max Weber simple identification of philosophy with
this science. When he discusses the ultimate conflicts in the greatest detail in order to use them as
ideal types for the purpose of scientific clarification
of religious-sociological reality, we see how particular
political, erotic, intellectual, and religious laws are in
discord and how they exclude each other. But this
entire view is expressly relative to a mere possibility:
The "intellectually constructed types of conflicts
among the 'orders of life' merely mean that in these
contexts, these inner conflicts are *possible* and 'adequate;'—surely *not* this, however: There is no kind

of standpoint from which they could be considered as 'abolished.' "[65]

Thus, the life aspect of an insoluble conflict among the possibilities in the world is an ultimate one for every scientifically oriented view, but it is not the last one for the consciousness of being in general. The rationally ultimate, from one point of view, is not the absolutely ultimate. When Max Weber speaks, he speaks sociologically; he limited this speaking only by limiting observations.

If we, therefore, concluded that by reflecting on the ultimate points of view we could develop a schema consisting of a mentionable definite number of value orders that show me, when I decide among them, where I stand philosophically, then this is not Weber's opinion. For him, all constructions are relative orientations, steps after which the path to further clarification lies open. For they are general, never sufficient for the reality of action in a situation. However, Weber mostly had a secret, sometimes overt, disdain for philosophical generalities.

So-called "ultimate viewpoints"? They produce silly talk . . . nothing else. And, above all: After very long experience and principled conviction, I have the viewpoint that only by putting to the test one's own supposed "ultimate" positional attitude on the

approach to sharply pointed, quite concrete problems, does his own real intention become clear to
the individual.[66]

Here philosophy is immersed in life; in concrete
situations it becomes the brightness of life becoming
lucid. But Max Weber stops right there in reflecting
about philosophy. He rarely interrupts his analysis
with a word about limits.

To this also belongs his awareness of recognizing
only empirical facts and causes in sociological research, but he did not wish to express their metaphysical meaning. He had a profound sense for the
cryptographical existence of things and had recognized Hegel and Burckhardt in their specific profundity from which they give us information about
the ciphers, but he did not set this task for himself
in science. "It is true that the course of humanity's
fate shockingly surges up in him who surveys a seg-
ment of it. But he will do well to keep his little
personal commentaries to himself, just as we shall
also do with our views of the oceans and the high
mountains. . . ."[67]

Max Weber did not philosophize directly; rather,
his philosophizing is to be sought in what he actually
did as a politician and scientist and as a human
being. It is real philosophy before its interpretation,

not cogitated philosophy as such which can apparently also be present in mere thinking without reality.

Max Weber as a Human Being

The phenomenon of Max Weber was *contradictory:* the commanding figure with his great gestures and enchanting eloquence, and, as far as the world was concerned, the anonymity of his almost obscure existence. His grace of movement, warmth of heart, and the childlike simplicity of his purely human interests—and an obscure relentlessness for truth, at moments intensified to the point of cursing the divinity.

The passionate research as will for knowledge which demanded every effort—and the indifference towards everything that was earned.

The constant movement into the apparent externals of technical research—and the close contact with the intrinsic truth of being.

The decisiveness of methodical knowledge—and the relativizing of everything that was known.

The cruel alienation in the concrete moment when the moral behavior of others disappointed him—and the unlimited kindness and forgiveness of wrongs endured.

The struggle against an opponent which breaks through all barriers—and the gallant readiness for conciliation at moments when victory seemed certain.

The agitation of his vision carried out through two decades of impending disaster—and the complete calm in the face of the catastrophe of 1918.

The capacity for the fortunate present, the sublime serenity of existence—and the boundless, annihilating anger.

The absoluteness in the fulfillment of moral demands of the law of the day—and the clairvoyant openness for the demons of the night.

Such contradictions are inherent in people as people; that they remain dominant, however, seemed to be indigenous to his *era*. Max Weber did not present himself as antithetical to his time, as if he were somehow above it. The era was, however, a time of disintegration. Glowing in his outward successes, splendid in his technical achievements and scientific findings, man had lost himself in them. Humanity had deteriorated among the machinery to such an extent that it no longer understood itself. Proceeding day by day in its ostentation, this world, with all its knowledge, was nevertheless ultimately without veracity. In such an era, greatness could not anchor itself to the beautiful form that would be visible and valid in a world which, having come to its senses, would have been able to be reflected in it. The time cried out for a strong personality, and was not able to use the greatest that it had. The consistency with which it eliminated Max Weber reveals something no longer shocking about the time itself. The discord between the world and existence certainly made him real for the era identified with this discord, but not in such a way that it would have recognized itself in him. Unaware of its own disunified state, it was devoted to covetousness, wealth, and success; it suffered only in individual situations, which Max Weber profoundly realized. He existed as an immortal man can exist alone in such times: breaking through all hollow forms, disclosing the origin of human existence! The fate of the time and the fate of Germany became real in a human being who was not a bystander, but rather, personified this fate and helped to bring it about. In torment and hope, he was like the beating heart of Europe on the brink of losing its intellectual and human life.

To others, Max Weber was an orientation and standard, not a model. Standing at the frontier of time, a human being can inspire but not mold others. His veracity commanded him, the mightiest person alive at that time, to reject all disciples; weaker persons behaved as if they were leaders and assumed prophetic attitudes. It would have been easy for him

to have a following of a sort, as many others of his
time had, but he faced everyone as an equal, on an
equal level, and nipped in the bud every kind of
emulation and discipleship.

Max Weber's essence seemed to stand between a
vanishing and a rising era. He could consider himself
an epigone, as having already lived in an era that had
not yet arrived. But actually, being human was a
certainty to him, even without valid objectivity,
worldly stature, or monumentality:

> It is the fate of our time, with its particular rationali-
> sation and intellectualisation, above all, with its dis-
> enchantment of the world that just the ultimate and
> most sublime values have receded from public life,
> . . . into the brotherliness of immediate relations of
> individuals to each other. It is not accidental that
> our greatest art is an intimate and not a monumen-
> tal one, nor that today, just within the smallest
> communal circles, from people to people, pianis-
> simo, that something pulsates which corresponds to
> what previously passed as prophetic pneuma, like a
> raging fire, through the great communities and
> welded them together.[68]

If Max Weber, in an equally objective manner,
saw reality in *history,* where it also existed, a particular response was evident nevertheless, where he himself was concerned. The Jewish prophets—their soli-

tude—occupied him in the extreme affliction of the war years. Looking at Michelangelo's ceiling in the Sistine Chapel, he felt the first signs of recovery from his illness. Rembrandt's picture in The Hague, *Saul and David*, was strangely familiar to him. He was in agreement with the world of Aeschylus and of Shakespeare. He honored and respected the other world that has its zenith in Goethe. He liked the idea of an individual enduring and serving as a reflection of a collapsing era. When someone glorified Boethius[69] because he preserved his philosophical certainty with Roman dignity and Greek wisdom in the ruin of the sixth century, Max Weber concurred with unusual warmth.

Condemned in a disintegrating era not to use his strength or to squander it by chance, Max Weber took the path of conquering negative attitudes, content that his head remained clear and his heart alive when his strength failed him. It is on the *path of rationality* that a human being finishes something, not by resignation, inurement, endurance through his vital strength, or forgetfulness and isolation, but by suffering, experiencing, and bringing it to clarity. Reason, the source of being human, is a colorless element if we choose to contemplate it. It cannot itself be characterized when it lacks the definition of a particular character. When conceived in isolation, it is nothing but an empty picture, but as reality it is everything that constitutes human dignity. It is never complete in time, but is human only as an upward path. Its essence is to *become* more, not to be more originally.

This ascent in the will for knowledge occurs as the frank seizure of compelling certainty and orientation in the possible, but in such a way that it is not mere understanding that determines, subordinates, and concludes; rather, in the peripheral situations of existence, it is reason, emanating from the impulse for the essential, that directs understanding. Max Weber's investigations, thus, reach out infinitely and their cohesiveness is derived from the essential which concerns people as people. The openness for things—even for the irrational and antirational, so as to either master and assimilate it or to recognize it as the other—simultaneously produced his broad latitude and his proximity to every human being he met, even the strangest of them. The manner in which he tried to overcome boundaries everywhere, and sought clarity in which to act with good will, arose from his reason. But reason is freedom.

How Max Weber desired freedom in himself and in those around him as a condition of everything essential to him was the intangible element in the ever-varying connections of communication: debates, questionless understanding, and the silent grasping of that which established the deepest trust in him. Freedom in the world cannot be defined as a way of the spirit, idealism, liberalism, or Germanism. It is simply being human that is so often pined away, betrayed, and not even attempted and therefore, when it is actually encountered, it is experienced as a human being revealing himself, although it is possible for, and suited to, every human being as a human being.

This is why Max Weber did not become a leader to those who wished to be subjugated. The power of his reason awakened the power of reason in others. Weber did not act through aesthetic charms like authority, through the superiority of knowledge and ability, or through an obscure charisma, but rather by producing soaring self-awareness in others. He cannot be the subject of a cult, but rather can only be the rational human being for all who wish to be rational, free, and self-aware. He inspired courage in a unique way, because everyone should walk and be allowed to walk the path that Max Weber had walked thus far.

Max Weber held fast to eighteenth-century ideas that were later called liberal; everything that results from the possible freedom of the individual, the inviolability of his personal sphere of existence, human rights, and dignity. It was an equally burning concern to devise how the individual human being kept his rational being and personality in a bureaucratized, mechanized, and barbarized future, when the human masses on the plains of the Mississippi and Siberia were necessarily bound to estates and corporations.

When we glance at his era and ours then, in the process of general illusions and fanaticism in which irrationality was being consecrated by false prophets, deceived swindlers, and powerful despots, Max Weber was the indelible presence of reason.

However, in the process of intellectualization or the cheapening of reason into mere understanding, into baseless knowledge and sophistry that can only deny and destroy, Max Weber's humanity itself is the historical manifestation of reason.

Reason is impersonal; it becomes *human* through its movement in time. In historical situations it thus becomes the stimulus in the solidarity among people, in the struggle for justice, in the openness which sees its own limitation peripherally, and in the bold venture to be expounded by including it in reality as well as through opposition. An attempt to show Max Weber's human reason, by relating what he did, how he conducted himself, how he judged, and what he loved, would be inexhaustible. Although Max

Weber did not direct any "great cause" in the world or intervene in history, he did not keep himself aloof. What appeared small to others was rewarding for him. It was the element of good-fellowship, which others considered unimportant, that he seized vehemently and unconditionally. His assistance to everyone who needed him, his role as his friends' advocate, his concern for those securing postdoctoral lecturing qualifications, for joint scientific investigations, and his numerous vain attempts at political action—all these occupied a large part of his life. At every moment he returned from the expanse of his research activity to his present situation with the people he loved or respected. The full weight of his action lay here, whether what happened was great or small, for in the light of theology, it makes no difference whether one rules the world or helps a human being in his solitary need, provided it is really done with all one's heart.

Max Weber was far removed from obstinate indifference to the world; he did not permit his independence to become wished-for isolation. His integration into his profession and a students' society was a life to which he assented. For that reason, it caused him pain—though he dealt with it calmly—when illness forced his early separation from teaching and the faculty did not offer him continued membership through a seat and a vote in its councils, as was suggested by the government; or when, during the war, regular evenings of political discussion among a large number of professors were established, and he was not invited to participate. He was so far removed from vanity that he did not need to look down indifferently upon these little things.

If we expected that such an unconditional German had hated or ignored any foreign nation, we would be mistaken. He was passionately interested in their quintessence and fate, especially the Russian and Anglo-Saxon nations. During the war he had a gallant concern for every prisoner accessible to him and struggled with nationalistic instincts of hate and the fear of spies that prevailed at the time. To him, a human being was always simply a human being, endowed with inalienable rights.

Max Weber's struggle was a matter of justice. When a scholar was attacked unjustly and insultingly, when an unwarranted reproach was directed at Max Weber's publisher, or when an academic career was denied to a gifted colleague, a summons to him brought help. He despised anti-Semitism. Although to him all politics was under the primacy of foreign policy and national power, his conviction on social questions was of a rare reliability. Deeply affected by the social movement in the eighties and nineties, he never denied the claims of a human being as a human being. But Max Weber's struggle was without a will for power. Though he was very much aware of this, it was not realized in him. He did not exploit or consolidate any personal victory. Lacking in Max Weber was the intellectually permeated will for power that made great statesmen—Caesar and Napoleon, Cromwell and Bismarck—admirable but also made them intolerable as human beings.

Even his reason was without will for power. It limited itself. Absolutely obedient to the ethical laws of reason in the Kantian sense, he allowed his moral judgment to be limited by the reality of the people he encountered. To be sure, he made no compromise with moral judgment, but he always questioned it anew, demanding the absolute only of himself. Even as one who relentlessly exposes the facts, he did not judge others. However, he showed a silent intolerance towards servility and coarseness, but was only ready for struggle when a *cause* seemed to demand it.

On one occasion, Max Weber believed that a university lecturer[70] had publicly lied and was thus, according to Weber's convictions, a disgrace to the teaching staff. Others also suspected the lecturer of lying, but felt neither the sense of shame nor the obligation to bring the fact to light. Max Weber took the case to court. Even those close to him said

that he exceeded reasonable limits. Reluctantly
agreeing, one of them likened it to Niagara Falls
plunging into a wash tub. Others said, critically, the
whole thing was comical and that he would make a
fool of himself. Skilled and excellent in court, Max
Weber immediately became the intellectual leader
of the trial, attaining his goal of demonstrating the
truth. Recalcitrant witnesses betrayed themselves
against their will under his cross-examination, resulting in the lecturer's dismissal from the university.
The matter was resolved and the case became a
notorious scandal.

Risking humiliation by intruding to the point of
becoming ridiculous in order to save the substance
of being, even as the world closes in, was the expression of his awareness of responsibility to the historical present. One must attend to the here and now.
Letting matters slide, considering them small and
insignificant, is the path to non-existence and the
inner shattering of the world. He expressed a general
rule for human conduct: "Go about our work and
master the 'demands of the day'—humanly as well
as professionally. That, however, is plain and simple,
provided everyone finds and obeys the demon who
holds the threads of *his* life."[71]

One expression of his self-consciousness was the
scorn of his own actual prestige. At a time when
every educated person placed value on intellectual

achievement and had to justify himself by producing some work of his own, acquiring self-esteem through published books, Max Weber, although a true creature in the realm of ideas, regarded prestige with absolute indifference. At his death little written by him was accessible. His most outstanding works were concealed in periodicals. Marianne Weber made the treasure of his works, culled from scattered remnants, available in ten volumes. Max Weber did not like to write any "books." He reluctantly began to do this at the end of his life when the task he had set for himself seemed to demand it. He instinctively chose a form of writing that made him personally unrecognizable. Even here he stood on the boundary between two worlds: the passing one, in which objectivity alone mattered, which and that he himself respected as an achievement in others, and an approaching one, which views objectivity as technology in which the true remains an apparent mystery. We thus see expressed Max Weber's serenity not cognizant of itself vis-à-vis the research he passionately pursued at the same time: "What I do not do, others will."[72] The objective element is replaceable; the anonymous element in its historical relevance is being.

His disdain for prestige as a "wise" man and his method were also evident in Max Weber's language.

Max Weber: Politician, Scientist, Philosopher

His style can astonish on a first reading. Indifference towards the work in its linguistic form, composition, extent, and proportions harmonizes with his forcefulness of thought, precision in forming concepts, and accuracy in developing his thought.

Max Weber did not work on style. He wrote from intensive brain work and power of representation, but he did not polish. His style is often colorless, therefore, depending on the point at issue; nevertheless, something of his own self remains even then.

Regarding content, there are repetitions and digressions before a return to the subject, sometimes unnecessary enumerations, complex sentences, and incidental brainstorms.

Max Weber characteristically did not like to look at his manuscripts or even his printed works. He took no pleasure in the published work, considering that work only a step in his progress.

Because Max Weber was entirely concerned with his subject and never with the language, he involuntarily succeeded in speaking a truly original language: truly non-artificial sounds of the human spirit. Because he was formless at a time when writers, by taking pains with form, generally dressed their dull content in purple prose, the form he acquired was an authentic and adequate expression of really original thinking and embodied human existence.

In his language as in everything else, Max Weber was extravagant, unpretentious, and frank; he behaved as he really was at each moment in his objective discipline and his humanity without ever acknowledging himself to be a model. Max Weber thus lies naked. He dared to reveal himself and never ascended to an artificial plane of expression.

Belief and Truth

Max Weber never wanted to make common cause with ideological combatants; with them there is no sense in talking. Their fanaticism adheres to fixed subjects. He, on the contrary, canvassed for unlimited rationality which, in its vast movement, reaches a limit where it must truly be decided only through struggle. Viewed from this angle, the ideological combatants hold to illusions; they appear in their thinking as if they knew the whole picture. Entirety and totality—relatively justified like all categories— dominate the idol of reactionary thinking as well as the utopia of revolutionary thinking. Fanatic belief has lost its original reference to transcendence as well as its capacity for communication with others in its subjective view of the absolute image of being, in the confident consciousness of harmony, and in the certainty that things finally proceed correctly by themselves according to necessity, the will of the people, and the unquestionable certitude of its own rightness.

Whenever Max Weber stood erect against these floods of illusions, perversions, and suggestions, against the intellectual absolutisms, he stood no less against the belieflessness of nihilism. He might well have despaired, becoming a misanthrope in his isolation. His belief supported him, this plain, unknowing belief, which, from its deepest source, again and again responded positively, seeking and finding what was still worthy of love in all the decay and recognizing what is simply alien. Never had he wished not to live, and never was his life as such the ultimate for him. He had a deep dread of and respect for death in battle since it could give meaning to what we all otherwise must suffer only passively.

His belief grew as worse events happened. While events were apparently going well, he was the inexorable pessimist who wanted to rescue the inexorable pessimist. He became calm when disaster struck; something that *is* remains—the possibility—which will *become* again. We might call banal optimism what, in truth, is an indestructible, positive belief in the incessant struggle for essential being. When he could in fact find nothing in his Heidelberg valedictory address in 1919 that could truly create courage as a visible substance of German essence, whose countenance was now completely distorted, he then spoke of the German forests as enduring, as neither remote, monumental grandeur nor sentimental idylls, but as the potential of the German. This was being oneself in one's individuality at any given time, the quietude of reflection, the response to everything human. Again he acknowledged what he had done in good and bad times: I thank God that I am a German.

In spite of all reflection, Max Weber was naive. He questioned, investigated, and thought to the extreme, exceeding normally possible standards. But what was investigated and thought was, after all, ultimately the means in the hand of him who possessed it, and not being possessed by it, was something more than this. He continued experiencing, searching, and separating; but all separation was elevated to a unity no longer known, of his real self being. Nothing finally declarable remained but the content of belief still unshakeably present as a substance in all that he experienced and thought.

If we wish to express this belief in spite of everything, the mysterious words he spoke when dying prevail: "That which is true is the truth."[73] To us, they are not a tautology but a kind of magic incanta-

tion as the expression of an existence whose truth
recognizes the modes of knowledge, like knowledge
gained through experience only as a function of a
responsible process whose source and aim remain
unknown, though affirmed.

Max Weber's search for truth originally appeared
as a *struggle.* As a young man he learned in the
atmosphere of Treitschke[74] and Bismarck "that serious, conscientious work, unconcerned with results, solely in the interest of truth, is held in low es-
teem. . . ."[75] His struggle for the true subsequently
proceeded against those who desired conviction and
intrinsic value in knowledge as knowledge, but just
by so doing falsely mix valuation and knowledge,
decision and insight. It proceeded against those who
want absolute knowledge, thereby becoming insincere because all knowledge is valid only from a certain point of view and in certain respects. The struggle proceeded against the rationalists, because they
do not critically observe the laws of knowledge;
against the irrationalists, because they fail to recognize the meaning of knowledge and its irreplaceable
manner of seizing the truth. He struggled against
philosophical falsification, which conceals the
abysses in conceptual schematics for the sake of harmony. His elementary anger proceeded against this,
as he called it, cheap sentimental style. For that

reason, Weber was attacked for his relativism and his cold objectivity by those who alleged the impossibility of value freedom and expressed dissatisfaction with a value free science. But behind Weber's demands stands a passion for truth which, through clarity of each mode of knowledge, seeks to get all the more resolutely to the point not perceived through research but by acting and producing in the world. This value freedom refers both to the purity of research and to the originality of action. His sense of truth was as remote from the satisfied materialism of liberalism as from its optimistic belief in research. In his opinion, the self-responsibility of the free individual was an unassailable condition of all values in the world, and every form of coercion of conscience was rejected by him.

The effectiveness of an unconditional will for truth is evident in Max Weber's *investigations* in a unique way. Max Weber neither gave a self-description of history, nor was history remote for him simply as something else. He entered into it with eyes trained by the reality of his own present, but he, as though present in both simultaneously, saw it as another world. For this reason, the objectivity of his historical analyses concerns us directly and, therefore, results in the ambiguous arousal of all possibilities of valuation. Some thought that a secret glorification of asceticism he himself accepted was carried out in his investigations of Calvinism; others thought that in these investigations Max Weber's horror of modern mechanization was leading to the unmasking of its original essence. Both can apparently be established, and both are wrong. If we incorrectly believe that Max Weber is represented by the admiring affirmation of these phenomena in this treatment of Calvinism, the Jewish prophets, the great demagogues, and so on, then we immediately notice the twilight everywhere they appear. The deeper Max Weber engages in research, the more intense this twilight becomes, so that upon thorough examination, we do not know whether Max Weber affirmed or denied while valuing. The essence of human action itself seems to exist through the boundless justice and freedom of vision of this scientist. He does not weigh and does not grant what is half right and wrong, but without general valuation shows what happened as historical necessity in its source, becoming visible in its possibilities and consequences. In these investigations a deeply hidden valuation of existence, which would always be proclaimed false in rationally valuating principles, is indirectly communicated.

Floundering

Max Weber was a great political writer, the founder of present-day sociology, a recognized scientist and author of extraordinary works, a companion to his wife, and a friend to his friends: a human being who knew happiness. But, political action was denied him, his works remain gigantic fragments, and his existence for many years was vitally shaken and narrowly limited in its effect.

A perspective that regards as mere fact Max Weber's floundering in the externals of his existence does not touch upon the true meaning of his essence. In a deeper sense, there was an atmosphere of floundering about him. His floundering is not identical to what he was unable to do, nor is his achievement identical to what he was able to accomplish. His floundering was a suffering akin to an active will—the true floundering of a human being in his imposed historical relevance.

In the *political* realm, the simply uncompleted determination of his being became engulfed in pure possibility. His political insight was that of Cassandra, convincing no one and, therefore, changing nothing, only suffering himself. Robbed of great influence, he resembled Machiavelli or Mirabeau,[76] achieving the political insights of the time with the same unmerciful realism, but he had character, the lack of which was denied them in human respects. He desired the highest goal: to act politically by reason of his reputation, without his own will for power. His floundering was essential because he wanted what was humanly true, but actually impossible.

In *research* he produced work that remained fragmented; not because he lacked strength, but for the sake of the truth, in keeping to the task. He felt himself floundering because of his boundless knowledge, because it is the purport of knowledge to flounder at the boundaries in order to set free the expanse for deeper truth in action and existence. He *sought* the point where floundering becomes that which is true. Incompleteness is the essence of science; in it, an extraordinary fragment is greater than any apparent completion.

In *philosophizing human existence* he suffered the limits of finiteness; with all the reality of his action he floundered outwardly, lacking an adequate sphere of activity and historical relevance of what had succeeded. He sought objectivity, what was whole and valid in the world to which he wanted to devote himself in order to really be himself, and he had to feel thrown back upon himself and excluded from the broad present in order to point to himself, like one who is taken from the world and space. But for him, this floundering was no floundering. He never weakened, but wherever he was, he grasped the task at hand with the full impetus of his existence. The very fact of this action, whether he encounters small or large spheres of reality where this full impetus occurs, only reveals relativity at the limit and even shows its symbolic character and becomes indifferent. This was his true floundering in the sense of returning to the source.

If Max Weber floundered in every objective sense that his standard disrupted, then this floundering is just like the appeal of truth. If Max Weber floundered in the ultimate inner meaning of man, that which emanates beyond the intimacy of good times with his neighbors and reliable loyalty, then as a human being Max Weber is the shining source of the eternal present and the fulfillment of the smallest things, because here exists the possibility of everything.

What he was as a human being cannot be comprehended if we subsume him under a psychological, sociological, or historical type. Those who called him an outsider, a presumptuous subjectivist, a liberal, a nationalist, or a democrat, who made him a representative of the individualistic bourgeoisie by whom he was shoved aside and a prototype of an era, as it was characterized, to which he was in opposition, or those who saw in his case a predominant asceticism, a heroic skepticism, or finally, without reverence for true fate and greatness, spoke of his escape into heroism, the most sublime form of shirking—are all mistaken. Through his own research and logical reflection, Weber struggled against the method of subsuming people and intellectual realities under general concepts of era, of classifying them according to their place in the history of ideas, or the method of distribution among contrasting pairs which apparently are sharply characterized; he understood these as cheap talk devoid of genuine value of recognition, as labels, as intellectual barbarism. This method can least of all be applied to him. Those who do so believe they can analyze him and rob themselves of viewing him in his depths, which depends on seeing through this man the source of human potentiality, or catching sight of what man is in the temporal phenomenon.

They likewise err who take him as a leader and prototype. Scarcely has another great human being declined to be so radical. We must grow with him. He is our indelible conscience that we seek and find that which is true for ourselves in communication, not to recite and admiringly accept the ready-made. In floundering he extends the torch, freedom to freedom.

The human being born into the world of Homer and the Jewish prophets did not lose himself in Nietzsche. He has his last great figure, for the present, in Max Weber, a figure of our world, which is being transformed at such a frantic pace that the special contents of the Weberian world have already passed away despite the brevity of time, though the fundamental questions of human existence, the ability for knowledge, and the decisive tasks remain. We no longer have a great man who could bring us to our senses in this manner. He was the last. We can still orient our lives, therefore, by looking at him even now that he has begun to slowly glide back into history. Only for those who knew him when he lived was he a presence; however, for posterity, which is looking for the German people in their true freedom, he is the possibility to be attained.

Antiquity, amidst a levelled and beliefless world, supported the individual in stoic philosophy. For philosophy, Socrates was the way because as a real human being he had been, done, and suffered what philosophy sought to understand throughout the centuries. In the world into which we are entering, a time of mass accumulation and mass rule, the utilization of everything, of crushing misery and banal happiness, it will again be the task of the individual to philosophically seek his truth. No objectivity will teach it to him. Perhaps he will become inspired, addressed by the open secret of a human being such as Max Weber. If this happens, however, we may say: Whoever understands floundering and death can come nearer to him. He will, however, remain incomprehensible to one who, while enjoying the beautiful world Max Weber also enjoyed in patient serenity, forgets death.

Max Weber: Concluding Characterization

(1960–1961)

Introduction

You may wonder:[1]

I am reporting on Max Weber's political thought which, after all, may not be a philosophy.

I have previously reported—although much more briefly—on Max Weber's science—which also may not be a philosophy.

My reasons are: 1. Philosophy that does not become political is not a genuine philosophy. Man stands the test of his philosophy in political thought and in concrete attitudes towards life situations. It has always been so.

2. Philosophy that does not have to do with the sciences, which presses towards science, and becomes evident in science is also not a genuine philosophy. Thus it has always been.

Politics and the sciences today are transformed so

radically that they only become clear, in view of world history, in the profundities of the transformation.

As I said anticipatorily, I have not made the philosophical literature of our time a theme but rather the philosophy of the present in the seriousness of its existence; not the hobbies of troublesome and diligent conceptual pastimes, but the thinking that takes hold of us in our possibilities as individuals and in the nations that originate in us.

Now here is a subjective statement.

Max Weber seemed to me the real philosopher of his time, the philosopher who did not explicitly state his philosophy, but lived and thought from it.

Such an assertion cannot be demonstrated as generally valid. It can be objected that the man is not at all so great, I [just] took a fancy [to him]. I think that those who speak in this manner have not really studied Max Weber.

1. For my part, I can only refer to my continuity of opinion over fifty years, and to the fact that over all these years, I never philosophized without thinking of Max Weber. I asked, What would he say? in adopting his basic position—not to continue his sociology and sociological research, but to make this philosophizing conscious.

I have been under his influence since 1909.

Max Weber: Concluding Characterization

When he died in 1920, I felt as if the German world had lost its heart, and as though it were no longer possible to continue living as we had until now.

I expressed this in a speech[2] given shortly after his death at the commemorative service arranged by the Heidelberg student body and in a booklet in 1932,[3] at the time when to speak of Germans was a dreadful noise, shortly before National Socialism's seizure of power, which induced my subtitle: "German Essence in Political Thought, in Research and Philosophizing" as an exorcism against that time. I later omitted the word "German" [and] only [wrote]: politician, scientist, philosopher. . . .

2. The following discussions can be attempted objectively.

a) Fame and historical effect.

Today, fame can be very great and at the same time very transitory. The process of forgetting begins soon after the death of a man. It is astonishing for everyone who has consciously witnessed half a century to see how names once famous and constantly talked about have completely disappeared.

Historical effect begins with an intellectual rebirth after death. The merely personal, interesting element has fallen away. No private relationship works any more—only the work, in its objective sense, matters to the new generation.

In this sense, Max Weber is alive even today, unlike most of his contemporaries.

Interest in him [can be] observed to grow in America and England today.

b) Whatever we see, we may attempt to demonstrate.

When, however, someone sees a notable, in the course of long meditation and realization, by virtue of real contemplation of the intellectual personality in connection with its actually increasing (though still very limited) effect in the world, and, above all, from the comprehensive intuitive perspective of the scientifically accomplished person, then one may demonstrate and establish that fact.

c) It is a matter for a contemporary (at least for my age).

We cannot know which effect is still taking place. I believe in seeing that it comes and that it is necessary; in any case, however, Max Weber was the representative personality for a main feature of our era that [is] true, honorable, and valid over a long time.

Max Weber in Philosophy Today

Today, in the skepticism towards philosophy that leads to actual scorn (only respecting it traditionally for form, where, in fact, philosophy must be born anew)—in this transition in which the linkage to the obvious and to the illusions and fictions of our expanded talk has brought philosophy, in the forms delivered, to withering without creating a new, conquering and valid form—there the phenomenon of Max Weber can be effective. It is effective by the fact that it, as a phenomenon in the extent of his thinking, in the greatest creations of intellectual intensity in the humanities, history, sociology in our time, in the ways of his political thought, in the actuality of his life and private existence, acts just then so philosophically, because it dispenses with speaking directly about the center and about philosophy in its origins.

With Max Weber, philosophy appears in its concrete effect, in the sciences and politics and the practice of living.

These thereby acquire a different character than usual, but which they have always had in all great philosophy. The sciences, politics, and the practice of living are often lost today in their obviousness, their ultimately aimless process, into the mere "further" in their operation, whenever they do not come from a philosophical center.

Science

Causal-empirical analysis up till now was almost always limited in that relatively justified principles of research were made absolutes; almost always confined to research itself, while research and valuation, knowledge, and volition were not separated; and almost always constructions of the real.

But Max Weber has advanced research in sociology and history so far and has raised the demands on research so high that those coming after him hesitated to follow him on this path.

[To] find this work that lies like a granite block in our path, which we must climb with the total strain and effort of reflected research, and to find the view to the correct path from it, we prefer to circumvent it, getting lost in the multiplicity of all possible erroneous paths without a view, in infinity, and in dead ends.

The big question: Can science attain a height to which those following cannot follow?

But the only fruitful and great path of perception is connected to the will to take this effort upon oneself.

To see this is also good, in case it is not successful, but the standard is there by which we know what to do; perhaps, after all, it acts in the service of those, preparing materials for those who are able and who dare to take the great process further.

The fork in the road lies here for every modern sociologist and historian: whether to adopt it or circumvent it.

The sensation, the symbol, the slogan, and the controlling prediction is missing.

Forgotten is the personal appearance of Max Weber at congresses, or discussions in political plenary sessions, but how few understood the subject itself, which he recognized and believed he had recognized in modesty, quietude, and far-reaching work.

Max Weber's life and thought were insolubly entwined. That, however, is presumptive in his case and presumes the nature of the subject.

He carried on expert scholarship as an objectively valid action that had value in itself. But it was, nevertheless, something relative to him that provided the means, that does not itself become absolute. He was aware of it, therefore, as a profession he took aesthetically seriously, in which he did not lose himself, despite his energy. The subject exists in itself; the person is indifferent. His sentence is valid: "What I do not do, others will."[4]

Everything was pertinent to him, whether scholarship, research, or political knowledge. Personality can only grow whenever a person is completely turned towards the subject, not when he strives for it directly out of interest in personality, revolving around himself and becoming empty.

We can ask: Was a great existence expressed in research? Has inexorable thought stopping at nothing forcibly brought forth this existence? That is not a question of either-or. The statements belong together. The one is as true as the other.

He was a human being in whom formation, coming from knowledge and original experience and transplanted in perception, permeated each other in such a way that no grand image of a real philosopher is conceivable in our time. For the philosopher is a human being who thinks directly on the basis of existence and recognizes where he is going to, always referring to an unstated absolute, always expressing himself in terms of the finite.

Politics

1. *In his sociology Max Weber's political knowledge is undisputed.* Max Weber's practical political thought (and action) for the moment and for the progress of Germany is, on the other hand, controversial. His frequent, unerring aim in a given situation is undeniable. . . .

2. *The entire picture of the political proposals of*

Max Weber: Concluding Characterization

Max Weber through the decades: Imaginary, so far as the forces and foregone conclusions actually present at that time did not even wrestle with him, rather ignored or unconsciously stifled [him].

Real, so far as they would have been able to promote and very probably would have promoted the progress and well-being of Germany.

This advancement presumes, however, that the motives and knowledge of the participants concerned and the population would have been such that Max Weber's proposals [would] have received an active response.

It is not only a matter of individual proposals, but, in these cases, a matter of the political way of thinking, the magnitude, the dignity, the veracity, the seriousness—the view towards the realities, the visual estimate, and the sense for the more distant future in current action.

From a level of feeling, thinking, and volition, Max Weber surmised a people that did not exist.

He saw the necessity of political pedagogic work not accomplished by Bismarck and completely lacking in the Wilhelmian state since not even one representative statesman was visible. Weber could not afford it. He publically tried to initiate it only in the inaugural address[5] and, unintentionally, in a few essays. He only began to speak persistently during the war, from 1917.

Every time he spoke, it was not yet too late to do something, but every time, it was rapidly growing too late. The moment was missed.

Thus, from his youth, he watched the catastrophe step by step before it happened,—a catastrophe in which he, after all, did not want to believe.

3. *Max Weber's will to greatness:*

a) Against lowliness, insubstantiality, narrowness, anxiety, the unconditional will for safety, for the high goals of self-assertion that make human beings worthy of life and testify to what it means to be a human being.

b) For veracity with a view towards the actual, knowing the limits of all knowledge, for risk on the basis of always insufficient knowledge, thoughts of asceticism and sacrifice translated into the reality of politics.

c) Under these standards his arguments always in the background of this demand on himself and others:

Misunderstood in this decisive element, because the others do not want it that way.

The uncommon impression [he made] even on those who were incompatible with him, who hated him, for whom his existence was intolerable because it touched their conscience and demanded what they did not even want to see.

Max Weber: Concluding Characterization

The overwhelming power of the average person, who seeks the practicable.

The grotesque difference between his being and this ordinary niveau.

4. *Max Weber did not act.* The passion of his thinking was always directed to the moment and his situation, and the decisive element in him did not result in the passion of his own active engagement.

a) In his youth and vital strength, the thought never occurred to him. Although he became a scholar reluctantly, he nevertheless applied his entire, immeasurable strength to this profession and perceived the decision equivocably. He did not consider the profession of politician. To do so was actually hopeless for a commoner under hollow constitutions. The energy of revolutionary play-acting with which he could conquer the masses—who were thinking along completely different lines—did not become strong in him. He would have needed friends and followers for that and at least the beginning of an audience among the people.

Also, he did not publicly begin the struggle against the emperor—the person and the system—even though the thought occurred to him he never seriously considered it. . . .

b) After his illness in 1898,[6] he was, in any case, physically incapable of political action.

It is strange, tragic, and comical, whenever we approach him, to momentarily see the impenetrable, profound spirit flaming in the high objectives before silently letting him fall or again dismissing him.

He never experienced "the great hour" of being called the leader of big politics, but made himself available, modestly ready for every task.

He put his entire energy into petty matters since great things were denied him.

He did nothing to come to power; rather, he behaved in such a way as to make this impossible.

Is he, therefore, the failure who, after all, just cannot really perform since he is not equal to the most simple intrigues, to opposing stupidity, to the dull pressure of the average?

Does he have a refinement that fails to grasp at the decisive moment?

He was the pervasive insight into German politics, tasks, and possibilities. He was the pervasive truth that was not understood.

We cannot avoid the impression that, under the leadership of his manner of thinking, Germany's fate and that of Europe could have taken a good direction. Why was it impossible?

Weber was limited in his sympathy for Naumann,[7] whom he had to set straight on decisive points.

Naumann, prepared, humble, with good will and

receptivity to Max Weber, did not understand him at crucial moments.

Max Weber suggested what was clear and simple, as well as what was not "practicable," people and conditions being as they are.

The Entire Picture: The Futile "Nevertheless"

He was the reality of thought in which the short-sightedness, narrowness, indolence, and emotionality of current politics became simultaneously evident to the observer, as demonstrated by history.

"Realism," which regards the ordinary as the final, determining, and decisive element, which has in view momentary success and not long term effects, was against him—even in retrospect.

Is he the symbol that futilely illuminates the light of the human spirit, with its inclination towards decline? But why and whence does this light generally illuminate?

Is Max Weber's [light] "nevertheless" untrue, and, under the assumption of constant energetic tension of spirit, action, and plan, is his patience the path on which the "nevertheless" is finally victorious when his moment has come?

Or is the melancholic view of history valid, which

moves hopelessly to its end and had, as its best element, the knowledge of people not entirely ensnared
in it but able to hold their heads above the flood
waters?

One, like the other, is transitory. Every human
being decides for himself what the decisive element
is for him and what he ought to do; what "eternity"
means and what vain decay is.

The Entire Picture in Antitheses of the Internal and External

1. The image: A man who almost always sees and
expresses the politically decisive element (for a long
time more privately than publically—his political literary work is uncommonly small vis-à-vis his entire
work) in the empty space, with passion in solitude,
anger, bitterness, grief, and fright, and who, all
things considered, does not even have an effect on
the progress of things.

2. To know the bulk of burdensome stupidity,
custom, pathetic traditional feelings, satisfaction
and phrases, careless unpreparedness, and the irresti-
ble, not even as opponents in the struggle for attaining things [consider]—the man who appears unre-
strained, indeed disturbed to colleagues and many
friends, of whom they complain that he is always

making noise, whom they do not take seriously, who knows and tells the truth for the possible welfare of all, who, as the passage of time has shown, was right, but not like one who predicts disaster with unstinting pessimism and is right in the end but as one who positively states the paths and necessities and always considers up to the end the right course as still possible, nevertheless. . . .

His work is unique in our era as an accomplishment and creation in perceiving the field of historical, sociological, and political knowledge.

But the human being was more than his work, in contrast to most people today who accomplish something; their accomplishment is more easily able to grow today, due to the force of the connections bearing it, rather than to their own essential natures.

His great work cannot be adequately interpreted without philosophy. To directly think of this philosophy itself seems to impair it. Whoever might be able to do so would be within the real philosophy, in the form of thought that corresponds to our situation.

The Skeptics and Opponents of Max Weber

Was he, after all, ultimately a dreamer, a utopian— this man with his inconsiderate knowledge of the facts, with the brightest political thinking of the time?

Did he, who saw the tendencies of world events, nevertheless support a lost cause?

Some have seen him this way, either rejecting him as strange and intolerable or loving him but complaining about this Niagara Falls who plunges into a wash tub. . . .

Max Weber is in closest touch with reality in every way; no one has surpassed him in realism. Perhaps few have attained this realism in its versatility and openness. But, at the same time, this thinking, beyond all realism, becomes deeply rooted there, whence human reality acquires its content as human, constructive, and substantial, elevating itself in the real, overpowering itself.

Physiognomy and gestures were original with him. No affectation and pretense surrounded him. He merely took his stand without the protection of conventions and masks. He placed no importance on himself. His naturalness automatically put aside all illusion and surrendered itself to every possible attack. He was the phenomenon of a human being who was entirely a human being, who thought what was, and became experiential.

Max Weber's Philosophy

It is not necessary to justify my treating Max Weber as a philosopher.

Whatever philosophy may be presupposes itself, when it is defined; when it is not pre-defined as relevant, the thinker decides what concerns and inspires and speaks to him philosophically—whoever is a human being is at the same time a philosopher in the heightened sense. . . .

The philosophical traits of his science per se. The meaning of his logical and methodological discussions is philosophical and even belongs to traditional philosophy, thus the references to philosophy professors (Rickert,[8] among others).

The pathos to really know, to know cogently, therefore [means] no philosophy as objective knowledge with regard to contents and therefore, oral rejection of philosophy *per se*. Empty speculation—the system, was strange to him. He had consciousness. This form of philosophy had its greatness; it has actually passed away. He did not deny the possibility, but he did not see it as present. But the original impulse of perception ("that which is true is the truth"[9] stated at last mysteriously in delirium) did not take effect arbitrarily. To know what we know and not know what significance, which meaning, this knowledge has (therefore logical studies). . . .

Max Weber's Illness

[Was] Max Weber's illness no accident? His insight into politics was as bright and true before the illness as after it. But his philosophical sense deepened, the extent of his view led to the immeasurable. What would he have been without the illness?

But the illness absolutely hindered him in practical politics; only for brief periods was he physically capable of it.

Does highest knowledge presume illness?

Kierkegaard, Nietzsche, Hölderlin?[10]

Max Weber's illness, a fundamentally different one: He was a man unlike others; [he] possessed an originally powerful vitality. Illness overtook him, not from external forces but from within his constitution itself.

With "illness" the mundane disposes of the significant. Max Weber himself, his spirit, was not sick. No symptoms can be found in his work. Illness did not touch his personality; rather it was a physically vital neurological illness, not an organic illness but rather a curable, functional one, fluctuating incalculably. At the end of his life he was healthier than he had been before the illness.

The Limits of Max Weber

1. He did not strive for power; he did not compete
for leadership; he limited himself to the printed
word; he waited, ready to assume a task, but did not
take action; he had radical restraint in the consciousness of his nerves: "I make mistakes."

2. He refused to work out in detail and pronounce
his philosophical consciousness.

3. In science, especially in devising "value freedom," maybe he did not entirely see through "posi-
tivism" in the science of the spirit, extracting with
the right intention "that which is factual," more and
more clearly (i.e., the "sense that was meant"), an
insufficient logical penetration of what is "fact" in
history and the humanities.

How far we may bring him together with positiv-
ism (Troeltsch).[11] Troeltsch [was] in error despite
his bright view of Max Weber's greatness.

Max Weber's Floundering in Time

He was the heart of Europe. The most extensive and
brightest consciousness of real events was in him,
objectivized at every moment for the most precise
formulation. . . .[12]

This great man certainly seemed to represent the

greatness of his time, whenever it was not ripe for leading politicians. That is, then, the fact. Time is hardly touched by Max Weber. He lived unknown, ineffectually, because, measured by the possible and the proper, he effected only petty matters. This fact now seems to me itself a symbol. The time cried out for "personality." It ignored the greatest that it had.

Indeed, Max Weber never pushed himself, grasped at anything, or competed for anything. Time needs, as it seems, strivers who can do that. It asks for but does not look for men whom it wants to follow. It is, as it seems, characterized by the fact that it cannot make use of great men; for that reason it does not have them. One human being was still living within the capacity of the great figures of the past. He was able to say what *is*. We can hardly doubt later periods will regard his works and his existence as one of the essential phenomena of this era.

In his lifetime he was known, as were many others, as a professor and sociologist; indeed, wherever he appeared, he was an event whose entire meaning those present probably rarely understood. Fascinated, perhaps shocked for a moment, people forgot—with a number of exceptions to be sure—to reflect on what that meant. In grand solitude he was without need of a friend, in any case, not satisfied with imperfection, but yet he easily spoke with anyone to whom he granted any trust. His unpretentiousness was open to humanity; his friendly disposition would not only have refused, but regarded as fatal, any admiration or veneration. He hardly ever conceptualized it and lived by facts, ideas, and tangibles in instinctive wisdom. He limited self-reflection to an individualistic kind.

They could not use him—not the old monarchy; not the republic. During the war they strove in vain to obtain political activity for him, even if only minor, through Berlin connections. He was ready to work in Poland. His friends hoped in vain that he would come to the National Assembly in Weimar; the German Democratic Party to which he belonged also could not use him. For each individual case— there are yet many—contingencies can probably be cited; each individual case can be understood causally. But the consistency with which Max Weber was excluded has something grand about it that no longer rouses indignation.

It[13] seemed that events had to transpire in such a way that he had no effect: one instance is the reaction of his particular environment, the world of the universities. At a time in which honorary doctorates were proliferating in Germany he never received one, but remained what he was: doctor of jurisprudence.

Most scholars who knew him feared him. His mere existence was like a reproach.

Today, it is different. It only seems different. The president[14] of the present Federal Republic, in a public speech at Heidelberg, recently extolled Max Weber as the greatest German he had met. In Heidelberg his name is frequently mentioned [in conjunction] with this speech.

Whenever we note remarkable coincidences, it seems strange that providence itself did not let him come to action. It struck him with an illness that made public (even academic) effectiveness impossible for him, at least from 1900 to 1914.

I[15] cannot say what this fact means, only that it means something. Consistency—even in the negative, the uniformity of form, the image of its existence without a will to power, the lack of fashion and stylization, arising from its originality, from the existence of people—cannot be merely accidental. . . .

Observations on
Max Weber's
Political Thought

(1962)

To render my thanks to our jubilarian, I chose the common recollections of a great man whom we all have met in the period from 1910 to 1920.

I would like to show how Max Weber's political goal-setting for Germany changed radically in content with Germany's defeat in 1918, but that his political way of thinking still remains the same and is true today.

Max Weber prevailed as a nationalist and imperialist. In his inaugural address of 1895[1] he demanded overseas expansion. It meant much for Germany's trade in distant oceans "if the German flags waved up and down the coasts."[2] Why? When trade eventually comes to be completely controlled and limited, as opposed to a world commerce that is still free today, then, as he said in 1897, "nothing but power, naked force decides beyond the foreign market."[3] The fact that German workers still can choose to seek employment opportunities in the fatherland or abroad, "will, however, definitely cease to be true in the not too distant future. . . . The worker will then be exclusively limited to that nutritional latitude that capital and the power of his fatherland know how to create for him."[4] Such was thought in the era of colonialism and imperialism for a Europe-centric world. The powers whose words carried weight were the European national states, yet moreover, Russia and North America [the United States].

Given the world situation at that time, Max Weber felt that hard, clear, and sobering politics "is blown away by the serious splendour of national feeling."[5] His view of the importance of power and force was just as frank as his feeling of unity with the German nation. In the German nation, he self-evidently lived without question. It was the entire, great German world, established in the tradition of a millenium. What this nation might be, however, he never attempted to suitably express. Whenever he discussed the concept of the nation in all sociological directions, he showed its ambiguity, which did not help to establish German self-awareness.

He based the concept of the German nation on the state through which it had acquired its form and power at that time, as a political factor of first rank. Only through this state does the nation have political responsibility. Separating Potsdam and Weimar, he attributed to Weimar the malice of enemies and the political irresponsibility of the Germans and repudiated it.

Since it had fallen to Germany's lot to become a great power, thanks to Bismarck, it was now faced with the task pursuant to such power. Among the forms of life that will dominate the terrestrial globe, he later said during the world war, are others than that of Russian tyranny and Anglo-Saxon conventions; the weaker nations will hold Germany responsible. In 1895, however, he had said: "We must understand that the unification of Germany was a youthful prank which the nation committed in its old age and by reason of its costliness would have better left undone, if it was to be the conclusion and not the starting point of a German world power politics."[6] Heavier yet than "a sharpened social conscience . . ."[7] weighing on us is "the awareness of our responsibility before history."[8] We must prepare ourselves for the great decisions that will take place in the future, in the expanse of the earth. Our historical obligation can be discussed along with them. We must create the conditions in the German Empire so that the great statesmen who have grown to the task can be recognized.

During the world war he lived incessantly agitated in his passionate will for victory, or better, a stalemate in this European civil war. His attempts to bring this political necessity to recognition were in vain. In the catastrophe of 1918, however, he was surprisingly calm. It has now become " 'fate'. . . . And we can manage with 'fate.' "9

What now? From the first moment on, Max Weber thought politically of what was coming. What can the aim be now? What can possibly be done? As always, he demanded honesty in the new situation. The nation and every individual are pledged to the "self-discipline of veracity."

Truthfulness commands us to recognize that "our world power is irrevocably gone as a great state. . . . Germany's world political role is over: The Anglo-Saxon world domination . . . is a fact. It is extremely unpleasant. . . . America's world domination was as inevitable as Rome's in antiquity after the Punic War."10 This insight means that every attempt to change the situation can only bring about, to be sure, a moment of luster in the irresponsible game (even that was perceived by Max Weber toward the end of World War I), and must in fact always produce a new, yet more severe catastrophe.

With this defeat of the German Empire, the first thing that existed in Max Weber was insight, not his will. Will acquiesced to knowledge. But he had confidence in a German future under the conditions now stated, if our veracity keeps us free from all fictions.

The German nation is a prerequisite. The German people still live. He acknowledged it with the national impotence of 1918 to 1919. At that time, he indeed saw the "face" of the German people "so destroyed, unlike that of any people in a similar situation. . . ."[11] But he immediately defended the Germans against the fabricated "stab in the back" charges beginning to be made at that time. "The current cheap judgments are vile, unjust, and unkind, and are associated, by the supporters of the smashed irresponsible party, with the alleged failure of the people. . . ."[12]

What are we then? " One hundred and ten years ago we showed the world that we—and only we— were capable of being under the foreign domination of one of the quite great civilised peoples. We are now doing that once again!"[13] "For I believe in the indestructibility of this Germany. . . ."[14] At this moment the state no longer existed; there were just Germans. We can see "their quite fabulous ability, simplicity, objectivity, capability—not their reaching!—for the 'beauty of everyday life,' in contrast to the beauty of intoxication or the balms of others. . . ."[15] ". . . never have I felt being a German so much as a gift of fate as in these dark days of its shame."[16]

But Max Weber was never a "nationalist" in the sense of blind affirmation of this nation as it is, but rather in the claim on itself and on the people to become what they could be. This "nationalism" in its unconditionality, honesty, and sobriety was opposed to the average German nationalism which was pathetically without courage, unprepared for veracity, satisfied with presumed security and a stupid arrogance of emotions, but risked its life on command, in military obedience, and without its own moral risk. Max Weber abhorred this frivolous game of national ideas. For him, the "German ideas of 1914" were "a literary product."

Max Weber's national feelings can speak of Germans up to the limit of despair. He speaks of the "type of 'satisfied' German who cannot possibly tolerate not being with the 'victorious cause' at any given time, with his breast swelled by elevating consciousness as a realist politician,"[17] by the "ignorant Philistines of 'Realpolitik'. . . ."[18] In the middle of the war, as he once again sees masses of soldiers at the railroad station in Bebra,[19] he writes: "They are really only fit for anything when in uniform; then they look like something and are in their element," and "The Hohenzollern dynasty only knows the military form of power: command, obey, stand at attention, bragging."[20] He wrote to Harnack[21] in 1906: "Luther towers high above everyone else . . . Lutherism, in its *historical* manifestations, for me—I do not deny it—is the most frightening of frights . . .,"[22] and "the fact that our nation has never experienced the school of hard asceticism in *any* form is . . . the source of all that which I find odious in it (as I do in myself)."[23]

When the defeat of 1918 became fact, he considered the dignity of the German nation alone as the element to be saved at the moment. It gave him the standard of hope for the future. But what happened? The emperor fled to the Netherlands. Ludendorff[24] and the others were shunned when the victors demanded the extradition of the war criminals (so-called by them) for the purpose of delivering them to a court before which the purity of their motives and actions would be attested to and demonstrated, all to the embarrassment of the victors and saving Germany the humiliation of their extradition (the demand of which was finally dropped by the victors). Whoever acts in a politically responsible manner stands up for his cause unto death. The leaders whom the Germans had trusted were not able to be models in defeat. In none of them could the nation again be correctly recognized. They did not save the greatness of the German name.

But Max Weber always opposed all summary criticism of what was collectively German, and all irresponsible, hard-hearted censure with his "nevertheless" and "yet."

Now the Germans were in a new basic political

situation due to the lost war. Max Weber's political way of thinking demanded that an unconditional, supreme principle must support politics. Only then are sublime passion, sacrificial courage, and insight possible in action. This supreme principle is not a doctrine but rather, a historical substance of essence propagating itself. Up till now, it was the nation in its absolute sovereignty. Can it remain that? When Max Weber said that Germany's position as a world power was irrevocably gone and America's world domination inevitable, he added: "One hopes that it will *persist,* that it will not be shared with Russia. *This,* for me, is the aim of our future world politics, for the Russian danger has only been exorcised for now, not forever."[25] Max Weber expressed judgment with this statement, although inadequately, in passing, before he died in 1920. The meaning is: Today supreme insight is no longer that of the nation but of the solidarity of the free Western nations and their allies. Like the individual nation formerly, the historical substance of the common West (not a doctrine that, in the polymorphism by which it is expressed, is only a result) is now the highest principle of politics for the present, and is established in the unconditional self-assertion of a historical essence. Since 1919 a sensible German politics has been able to find the self-assertion of the nation solely through unconditional participation in the self-assertion of Western political freedom. As German counter-reason has deviated from this path, it has brought about disaster for the Germans and the world.

Reason in the political way of thinking demands knowledge. Accomplishing this, purely and candidly, is conditional upon the clarity of the political will. In order that the conceptions were not misleading through deception and self-delusion, Max Weber demanded the "value freedom" of science. Only with extreme striving for the scientifically compelling and perceivable comes the actual resolution of the emotional confusion and sophistical argumentation. Max Weber's aim in his passionate striving for objectivity was always to distinguish what one can commonly know of all other things with the intellect, from what is based on the decision of the will in conflict. Max Weber did not reach his aim, anymore than any human being will ever reach it. For in the reality of scientific thought itself, both elements are united. The difference among thinking people is only whether they assume the task of separating them as a constant disturbance or whether they reject them in favor of existential confusion. A report of a conversation between Max Weber and Schumpeter[26] that we know about through Somary[27] can serve as a symbol instead of an objective discussion, which would be impossible due to its

KARL JASPERS ON MAX WEBER

brevity. Both men had met Ludo Moritz Hartmann[28] and Somary in a Viennese café.[29] Schumpeter had expressed his pleasure about the Russian
Revolution. Socialism is no longer a paper discussion,
but must prove its viability. Max Weber excitedly
states that Communism in the Russian stage of development is flatly a crime; its path will extend beyond unprecedented misery and end in a horrible
catastrophe. "That may surely be," said Schumpeter,
"but that will be quite a nice laboratory for us." "A
laboratory piled up with human corpses," Max
Weber exploded. "There is also the science of anat-
omy," retorted Schumpeter. Attempts to change the
subject failed. Weber became more loud and vehement, Schumpeter, softer and more sarcastic. All
around the café guests listened curiously until
Weber jumped up with the words, "That can no
longer be tolerated," and hurried to the street, followed by Hartmann who brought him his hat.
Schumpeter, who remained behind, only said smil-
ingly: "How can a person shout so in a café?" This
is the question: In which frame of mind is value-free,
scientific objectivity being strived for? This question
is not being determined by any scientific knowledge.
My heart beats only for Max Weber and his magnificent "tactlessness," when he used to deplore such
things and even later—versus vile intellectualism—it
beats for his manner of pursuing science, without

forgetting human responsibility for a moment,—versus scientific equanimity, that sham image of transcendentally established calm. Some have charged that Max Weber's "value freedom" and his "objectivism" paralyze the mind, the will, and action. The opposite is true. But "value freedom" and the motives and paths to its realization are seldom understood even today.

Whatever aims are continually sought in politics, politics itself, if it is great and serious, is always based on responsibility. Max Weber's distinction between the principle ethic and the responsibility ethic does not mean setting free an unprincipled politics by relying on a responsibility ethic for politics. The responsibility ethic itself includes the conviction of responsibility for the consequences of its actions and readiness for every sacrifice, though not for something that would destroy the meaning of politics itself.

> . . . when a mature human being—whether young or old—who really feels this responsibility for the consequences with his full soul and who acts in an ethically responsible manner, says at any point: 'Here I stand! I can do nothing else'[30] [it] is immensely shocking. For, this position, to be sure, must be able to take place at some time or other for each of us who is not intrinsically dead. To that extent, the principle ethic and the responsibility

ethic are not absolute opposites, but complements, which together just constitute the authentic human being. . . .[31]

Max Weber did not accuse the world, the nature of people, or the German people. He despised such accusations by which the accusers, in summary and total judgments, consider themselves better and fall into folly: if what they suggested were done, then everything would be correct. He sketches the statesman in his greatness, from which he got the strength to assert his cause in opposition to the world, the strength to patiently "drill hard boards with passion and visual estimation simultaneously."[32]

Max Weber's politics of the serious saw through the politics of geniality, which was always anxiously disturbed. The self-satisfaction of those who considered themselves smarter than Max Weber and, despite this, admired him compassionately, is political perdition. It brings about industrious continuity, not borne by the political substance of great responsibility. It makes itself blind to the real threats that suddenly befall the catastrophes. It cripples the readiness to act towards them with the courage of truth. In the speech in which truth is mentioned, but where the point is always interrupted, nothing is basically taken seriously. A demand is not placed on truth itself and on fellow citizens; on the contrary, truth is deprived of its piquancy and therewith, also of itself. It is this miniaturizing of all things that causes the earnestness of a human being to disintegrate. Aristocracy and rank disappear and with them the talent for a great, redemptive politics.

No one was more realistic at that time; perhaps no one was as realistic in the particulars as Max Weber. But he distinguished between reality as an inescapable element and reality as an ever-present conception, opinion, and will of the people, which it is possible to change. The unlimited submarine warfare, which resulted in the foreseeable entrance of America into the war, was not necessary. Wilson's demand for the complete disarmament of Germany during the armistice, which rendered him impotent and caused the Treaty of Versailles to be dictated without his participation, was not necessary. In this, as in other cases, Max Weber said and saw in a moment what would happen before it happened. Germany did not accept the slow change in the way of thinking that defined his political education.

It was said Max Weber was unrealistic at the decisive point, despite everything; he demanded too much of people; he had to flounder because he required from people what they could not fulfill. The answer to this is: so long as the earnestness that was acting in Max Weber is condemned to floundering, so long as his great veracity does not cleanse thoughts and impulses, then will the condition remain that must, as such, lead humanity to decline in the foreseeable future. The demand is exorbitant because of the situation of the people, not because of the non-realism of Max Weber.

The Marxists' judgment that Max Weber was an exponent of the bourgeois class may be mentioned only incidentally. [They say] that is why his way of thinking was false. This reproach lacks any real agreement with objective events and realities. Max Weber considered himself to be in a situation where everything in political action depended on consciously belonging to the bourgeois class of his time. For him, that was not an unconditional belonging, because class was nothing absolute to him. The Marxist reproach had a truly destructive effect in the form of the brutal, actual power of the Marxists; intellectually it is superfluous and for a thinking human being, ridiculous. The answer would be Max Weber's sentence: "We cannot talk with ideological combatants." But he did talk with them, because the principle of his being was: We should be able to talk to each other under all circumstances. Even to bring the differences to clarity is only possible by speaking to each other. Whoever keeps himself open, whoever can be questioned about his own principles and actions, has the better chance of finding truth. Whoever secludes himself intellectually establishes the condition that is prerequisite to violence. It must be possible to speak freely, to reply with a challenge, to tentatively enter into a conversation that mutually inquires about assumptions and demands to examine assumptions—this is, therefore, his reply to the Marxist reproach.

A shocking criticism, which perverts Max Weber's political way of thinking, maintains that he set down the path upon which Hitler's Germany became a reality. His sociological concepts (perhaps the idea of the leader and charismatic leadership), like his political motives in the nationalism and imperialism of his time, as well as his realistic knowledge of the meaning of power and force, have reclined on the line to Nazism, so they say. His distinction between the responsibility ethic and the principle ethic has been abandoned in favor of power and force.

But to espy the devil, recognize him, and not close one's eyes to him does not mean that one becomes him. Did Max Weber perhaps consider power and force to be the highest aim? In no way. In a treatise he wrote about the meaning of value freedom:

In the sphere of *valuation,* however, one point of view is very meaningfully advocated, which would like to see the power of the state very much increased to the conceivable extreme in the interest of realising its means of coercion against resistance, but, on the other hand, which denies [the state] every *individual* value and stamps it as a mere technical expedient for the realisation of quite other values from which alone it could sustain its dignity in feudal tenure and therefore could only preserve it as long as it does not try to divest itself of this, its handyman's vocation.[33]

These sentences, expressed by Max Weber as a possibility, mean: In the reality of the world, that can only exist which has power and is secured by force if the occasion arises. The state is a necessity. Max Weber did not love it; rather he saw in it a strange monster. The state as a technical expedient, however, secures its life through the political responsibility of all its members. It fails in the process of following mere rules of the game, in administering and continuing to merely exist. It is destroyed by granting free play to technical expedients and to power *per se.* It becomes dead without the proud, independent will of the people sustaining it.

Max Weber's sociological categories could delude one who does not constantly seek to separate insight and will. His sociological category of "charismatic leadership" was meant to be value-neutral. Its fulfillment is the historical event that is being performed by people. It can neither be justified nor discarded by the sociological category as such. It can

appear strange that Moses, Pericles, and Caesar sociologically fall under the same category as Knipperdolling[34] and Hitler. But the judgment about them
does not arise from sociological knowledge, but
rather, from the political will and judgments. When
Max Weber was thinking of an authoritative democracy in 1918, he saw that no leaders were available.
They could only arise in a real democracy through
education in the political struggle; they could not
suddenly be there when one chooses to have them.
Max Weber would have been able to say, like Nietzsche: "The necessity of such leaders, the horrible
danger that they could fail to appear or turn out
badly—those are our real worries and despair."

Max Weber was not yet familiar with, and did not
even see the onset of, what would become real in
Russia and Germany in the period after his, as a
principle of total rule in a technical age. Total rule
is the negative mirror image of that which Max
Weber saw as the hard path towards the realization
of political greatness, for it is the end of politics as
envisaged by Max Weber. He lived in the continuity
of the political freedom of the Greeks.

Would Max Weber have assented to any German
state out of a sense of nationalism? It seemed so
when he said that it did not depend on the constitution or on the ruling class at any given time, but
rather, primarily on whether the political system

could bring men to the highest pinnacle of their political ability, then on whether it could make social justice and freedom possible. He struggled against the Wilhelmian state because this state impeded the ascent of competent politicians in a free democratic struggle and, therefore, brought the nation into the utmost danger. But this state, in its entire condition of life, still somehow held its dignity in feudal tenure within its sense of national reality without questioning and expressly discussing this. But what if Max Weber had lived to see a German state totally break from this relationship with feudal tenure? What would he have thought about the Saar plebiscite in 1935? It seems to me that Max Weber's theorem had lost its validity: [He is] indifferent [as to] which constitution to choose: First take care of the German state, be that as it may, and then take care of the constitution! This state was no longer held in feudal tenure by the German nation. Now it could only be a matter of setting the German nation free again in its dignity. The plebiscite was an act of struggle in this liberation. It could have represented the voice of the entire, violated German nation. I assumed at that time, therefore, that Max Weber would have agreed with that small minority in the Saarland who refused incorporation into the un-German empire governed by a band of murderers and their unsuspecting, culpable subordinates. Those are pure constructions, however, from Max Weber's way of thinking. He was not acquainted with the period of National Socialism. Perhaps it would not have attained power at all if Max Weber had been able to speak his mind in the years long before 1933, but that is unlikely. The Germans did not listen to him. Even today, his political thought receives very slight response.

What would have taken place in Max Weber if he had seen National Socialism? His despair over things German certainly would have infinitely surpassed all previous despair. But what would he have thought and done politically? He could not acknowledge a state as German that nowhere held its dignity in feudal tenure by the nation. For this *state,* though it would end inexorably with it, annihilated this *nation* step by step.

Would Max Weber then have altogether despaired of the German nation? Even if its countenance from 1933–45 was incomparably more desecrated than it had even been in 1918, if all that was abysmally vile had seized the efficiency of technical ability, and if what was still German had been killed or lay dormant—was not something left living, after all, that remained German? What if Max Weber had been forcibly annihilated as a sacrifice for what is German? We cannot know that. But it certainly seems to me that to despair of what is German, altogether and completely, for always and in every form, would not have been possible for Max Weber.

If the end of politics steps in; that is, the politics of free people in the process of fate, what happens? A condition in which the individual, without political dignity, in the expanse of existence left to him, may still realize what is externally displayed at every moment of destruction: the intimacy of personal existence in humanity among individuals, the perception of things, inner veracity, and steadfastness in decline. Politics is fate, even when fate is the end of politics. Politics is not the ultimate for people as people. When asked what he was thinking of, a high Prussian official on his death bed said: "Of the state." Max Weber's last words were: "That which is true is the truth."[35]

Excerpts from Letters to Hannah Arendt

(1966)

Dear Hannah,[1]
  It is quite different with Max Weber. He was really serious about boundless honesty. He was a modern human being, therefore, who, in the face of absolute confusion, completely exposed himself to power struggles and permitted no kind of secret cheating, by living passionately and struggling aimlessly with himself. He felt science, in its entirety, to be completely unsatisfying in fulfilling life. He acquired this usually suppressed meaning from the Old Testament: that God was not only experienced in the covenant as law-giving and merciful, but evil like a devil. Whoever does not think in theory like Max Weber, but realizes this concept of being human, indeed can attain wonderful heights, but just for a moment, because everything becomes questionable. He had an inclination for dying, therefore, all his life, an impulse for suicidal thoughts. Ricarda Huch[2] considered him an actor. A young man from the Mommsen family recently wrote an important book about Max Weber's politics[3] (important, because of many new sources), and established his political thought on contradictions in concrete judgments,

characterized him as a representative of imperialism, and declared his way of thinking a path to Hitler. Last year on the occasion of Max Weber's 100th birthday celebration there was endless talk about small matters, devoid of any meaning for this man. I think about him very much because of his "independent thinking," whose meaning I would like to illuminate in my correspondence with you, but, up till now I am only getting into a multiplicity of subjects and right now I have completely stopped (due to fatigue and pain). I would still like to finish the book and I am not completely giving up hope, even though I have not made progress for weeks, except for occasional notes. Once again, Max Weber: although not a genius and inferior to both Nietzsche and Kierkegaard, he is, nevertheless, simply a man *vis-à-vis* these eternally young and dubious people. And that, even physically. They were all sick, but Max Weber in a different way: it was neither paralysis nor schizophrenia, but something undiagnosable up till now. Elementary, somehow biologically based phases were in his life: highest capacity for work and accomplishment, and then collapse during which he could not even read any more. During the last year of his life, he was in a "manic" but fully disciplined state of mind—we saw him in Heidelberg two months before his death on the occasion of his last visit. He said that the sentences and concepts had never flowed from his pen with such clarity and unceasing continuity and vehemence (the famous 170 pages that begin *Economy and Society* demonstrate this). He was an inconceivably prolific writer, gave lectures which no student has forgotten. He constantly took political trips and gave speeches, beaming and suffering at the same time. This suffering seemed immeasurable. If he had lived, he would probably have collapsed anew. Finally, there was his conscious dying, completely calm, rejecting any contrition, with the words: "That which is true is the truth."[4] I still see him [in my home,] as he got up on tiptoe, speaking imploringly in the room, standing before Gertrud, relating an overt family untruth, because Gertrud had hit a nerve with a question about Alfred Weber.[5] Upon leaving when it was dark, he spoke his parting words, which were always encouraging to me, on the occasion of my *Psychologie der Weltanschauungen,* just published.[6] I told you about it previously. It was as if he never forgot anything in the last months of a life that exceeded all boundaries, not even small human considerations. . . .

Yours,
Karl

Basel
16 November 1966

Dear Hannah,

1. I have not expressed myself about *Science as a Profession* in the 1919 dispute. It did not seem worthwhile. The George-world[7] primarily stated its unpleasant viewpoints, just as devoid of understanding of science as arrogant in judgment. It was no discussion.

2. I probably told you on occasions how, immediately after the publication of *Science as a Profession*, Max Weber, Thoma,[8] and I were sitting together on a Sunday afternoon in the garden of the magnificent house on Ziegelhäuser Landstrasse.[9] Naturally, we were talking primarily about the speech that was extraordinarily stimulating at that time. This speech was hard, inexorable, and moving.

Perhaps I said: You are not saying a word about the meaning of science. If science is just what you say about it, why are you occupied with it? I spoke about Kant's "ideas" and the fact that each science only preserves its meaning, which itself proceeds beyond science, through an idea. Max Weber hardly knew anything about Kantian ideas and did not react to them. Finally, I said, facing Thoma: "He, himself, does not know what meaning science has and why he is pursuing it." Max Weber winced visibly: "Well, to see what we can withstand, but we'd better not talk about it."

3. The value judgment discussion before 1914 stirred up the intellectual world at that time (first, at the sociologists' congress) in a way hardly known. It was felt that something threatening was evident there. It seemed as if the humanities, as they were then being pursued, were in danger of having to be substantially changed. There was a restlessness about the self-assertion of genial scientific objectivity, which was partly unmasked for its appearances.

It is characteristic that a few people (Oncken,[10] Spranger,[11] and others) decided to hold a "secret meeting" with Max Weber in order to perhaps arrive, within the self-discipline of a small circle of trusted scientists, at the aim of a better understanding. This was reported in the history of the Society for Social Politics, published in the thirties, after it was disbanded (I think the report was written by its last secretary, Boese).[12] At the end of this meeting, Max Weber sadly said: "They, nevertheless, do not understand me."

4. In fact, the aim of an objective, logical understanding alone was not attained. It makes a demand that is unrealizable; if they choose to acknowledge it, and thereby to get on a new path of neither wanting

nor understanding the demand. Perhaps the highest task of humanistic, sociological, psychological, and historical knowledge is expressed in it. It deals not only with methodology, but rather, with the vital condition of the life of the perceiver himself.

5. Whenever I spoke to Max Weber, I was always very shy, not really conversing; rather, I sometimes risked asking immoderate, even impertinent questions (a few sentences I heard from him became the key to Max Weber for me). I thus said at the time: All understanding is inseparable from valuations. What you want is very simple using Galileo: that the circle is not more noble than the ellipse; I can accomplish that without further ado. But you want to separate what obviously must be separated in a completely different way, because it actually always remains connected. The highest state can be attained by a "suspension of valuation." But, how do we accomplish that?

Max Weber did not agree with how I may have expressed that at the time. In his speech the problem seemed simpler than it is, but in reality, he has profoundly experienced it when the unsolvable itself is pushing more and more intensely towards the solution, through tension in itself, on the way to the infinite. That changes the content, mood, and meaning of all that research. If we have become audibly acute, we feel it almost in Max Weber's entire works,

which are fundamentally different from other works
with the same theme. . . .

Yours,
Karl

Notes

Introduction

1. *Allgemeine Psychopathologie. Ein Leitfaden für studie-ände Ärtzte und Psychologen* (Berlin: J. Springer, 1913), trans. J. Hoenig and Marian W. Hamilton as *General Psychopathology* (Chicago: The University of Chicago Press, 1963).
2. Karl Jaspers, "Philosophical Autobiography," in *The Philosophy of Karl Jaspers*, ed. Arthur Schilpp (New York: Tudor Publishing Co., 1957), p. 33.
3. Ibid., p. 34.
4. *Die Schuldfrage. Ein Beitrag zur deutschen Frage* (Heidelberg: Verlag Lambert Schneider, 1946), trans. E. B. Ashton as *The Question of German Guilt* (New York: Dial Press, Inc., 1947).
5. Despite these and other developments, Jaspers felt that the question as to why he and his wife left Heidelberg for Basel cannot be answered. See Jaspers, *Schicksal und Wille. Autobiographische Schriften*, ed. Hans Saner (Munich: R. Piper & Co. Verlag, 1967), pp. 164–83.
6. Jaspers, "Philosophical Autobiography," pp. 85–86.
7. Jaspers, "Reply to My Critics," in *The Philosophy of Karl Jaspers*, pp. 854–55.
8. Jaspers, "Max Weber. Politiker, Forscher, Philosoph," in *Aneignung und Polemik. Gesammelte Reden und Aufsätze*

zur *Geschichte der Philosophie,* ed. Hans Saner (Munich: R. Piper & Co. Verlag, 1968), p. 425.

9. Jaspers, *Schicksal und Wille,* p. 33.

10. Jaspers, *Psychologie der Weltanschauungen,* 4th ed. (Berlin: Springer-Verlag, 1954), p. 357.

11. Jaspers, "Philosophical Autobiography," p. 32.

12. Ernst Moritz Manasse, "Jaspers' Relation to Max Weber," in *The Philosophy of Karl Jaspers,* p. 391.

13. Jaspers, "Reply to My Critics," p. 855.

14. Ibid.

15. Jaspers quoted in Marianne Weber, *Max Weber. Ein Lebensbild* (Tübingen: J. C. B. Mohr (Paul Siebeck), 1926), p. 580.

16. Jaspers, "Philosophical Autobiography," p. 58.

17. Jaspers, *Schicksal und Wille,* p. 166.

18. Jaspers, *Philosophy Is for Everyone: A Short Course in Philosophical Thinking,* trans. R. F. C. Hull and Grete Wels (New York: Harcourt, Brace & World, Inc., 1967), pp. 51–52.

19. Jaspers, *The Future of Germany,* trans. and ed. E. B. Ashton (Chicago: The University of Chicago Press, 1967), p. 15. For a review of the German edition of this work, see my review in *The Academic Reviewer* 2 (February 1968): 5–6; also my review of Jaspers, *Antwort zur Kritik meiner Schrift 'Wohin treibt die Bundesrepublik?'* (Munich: R. Piper & Co. Verlag, 1967) in *The Academic Reviewer* 3 (January 1969): 12.

20. Weber quoted in Marianne Weber, p. 665.

21. Ibid.

22. Ibid.

23. Jaspers, *The Future of Germany,* pp. 60–66.

24. Ibid., p. 78.

25. See the collection of essays and speeches in *Freiheit und*

Notes

Wiedervereinigung. Über Aufgaben deutscher Politik (Munich: R. Piper & Co. Verlag, 1960) and *Hoffnung und Sorge. Schriften zur deutschen Politik 1945–1965* (Munich: R. Piper & Co. Verlag, 1965).

26. Jaspers, "Philosophical Autobiography," p. 64.
27. Ibid.
28. This information was supplied to me by Dr. Hans Saner, personal assistant to Jaspers from 1962 until 1969, in his letter of 17 May 1978.
29. Jaspers quoted in Martin Green, *The von Richthofen Sisters: The Triumphant and the Tragic Modes of Love* (New York: Basic Books, Inc., 1974), pp. 172–73.
30. This portion of the letter, which does not appear in the printed excerpt, was provided to me by Professor Eduard Baumgarten, nephew of Weber, in his letter of 1 April 1978.
31. Quoted in Baumgarten, "Zur Erinnerung an die Jaspers'sche Form, Streitgespräche—feindlich und freundlich—fort und fort in Gang zu halten," in *Erinnerungen an Karl Jaspers,* eds. Klaus Piper and Hans Saner (Munich: R. Piper & Co. Verlag, 1974), p. 125.
32. Information provided to me by Dr. Saner.
33. Jaspers, "Philosophical Autobiography," p. 29.
34. Weber, "Wissenschaft als Beruf," in *Gesammelten Aufsätze zur Wissenschaftslehre* (Tübingen: J. C. B. Mohr (Paul Siebeck), 1922), pp. 530, 534.
35. Jaspers quoted in Hans Saner "Zu Karl Jaspers' Nachlaß," in *Karl Jaspers in der Diskussion,* ed. Hans Saner (Munich: R. Piper & Co. Verlag, 1973), p. 449.
36. Weber, "Wissenschaft als Beruf," p. 531.
37. Jaspers, "Max Weber. Politiker, Forscher, Philosoph," p. 428.
38. Weber, "Wissenschaft als Beruf," p. 548.

Max Weber: A Commemorative Address (1920)

1. *Die römische Agrargeschichte in ihrer Bedeutung für das Staats-und Privatrecht* (Stuttgart: Ferdinand Enke, 1891) and *Die Börse* (Göttingen: Vandenhoeck und Ruprecht, 1984).
2. Quoted in Marianne Weber, *Max Weber. Ein Lebensbild* (Tübingen: J. C. B. Mohr (Paul Siebeck), 1926), p. 701; trans. and ed. Harry Zohn as *Max Weber: A Biography* (New York: John Wiley & Sons, 1975).
3. Aside from the already cited works, the others are: *Die Verhältnisse der Landarbeiter in ostelbischen Deutschland* (Berlin: Duncker & Humblot, 1892); *Zur Geschichte der Handelsgesellschaften im Mittelalter nach südeuropäischen Quellen* (Stuttgart: Ferdinand Enke, 1889); "Die sozialen Gründe des Untergangs der antiken Kultur," *Die Wahrheit* 6 (1896): 57–77; trans. R. I. Frank as "The Social Causes of the Decline of Ancient Civilization," in *The Agrarian Sociology of Ancient Civilizations* (Atlantic Highlands, N.J.: Humanities Press, 1976), pp. 387–411; "Roscher und Knies und die logischen Probleme der historischen Nationalökonomie," *Schmollers Jahrbücher für Gesetzgebung* 27 (1903): 1181–221: 29 (1905): 1323–84: 30 (1906): 81–120; trans. Guy Oakes as *Roscher and Knies: The Logical Problems of Historical Economics* (New York: The Free Press, 1975); "Kritische Studien auf dem Gebiet der kulturwissenschaftlichen Logik" *Archiv für Sozialwissenschaft und Sozialpolitik* XXII (1906): 143–207, hereafter cited as *Archiv;* trans. Edward A. Shils and Henry A. Finch as "Critical Studies in the Logic of the Cultural Sciences," in their edited work *Max Weber*

Notes

on the Methodology of the Social Sciences (Glencoe, Ill.: The Free Press, 1949), pp. 113–88; "Rußlands Übergang zum Scheinkonstitutionalismus," Archiv XXIII (1906): 165–401; "Rußlands Übergang zur Scheindemokratie," Die Hilfe, 24 June 1917, pp. 272–79; "Zur Psychophysik der industriellen Arbeit," Archiv XXVII (1908): 730–70; XXVIII (1909): 219–277; XXIX (1909): 513–42; "Die protestantische Ethik und der 'Geist' des Kapitalismus," Archiv XX (1904): 1–54; XXI (1905): 1–110; trans. Talcott Parsons as The Protestant Ethic and the Spirit of Capitalism (New York: Charles Scribner's Sons, 1958): "Die Wirtschaftsethik der Weltreligionen," Archiv 41 (1915–1916): 1–87, 335–421, 613–744; trans. H. H. Gerth and C. Wright Mills as "The Psychology of the World Religions," "India: The Brahman and the Castes," and "The Chinese Literati," in their edited work From Max Weber: Essays in Sociology (New York: Oxford University Press, 1946), pp. 267–301, 396–415, and 416–44, respectively; "Das Antike Judentum," Archiv 44 (1917–18): 52–138, 349–443, 601–26; 46 (1918–19): 40–113, 311–66, 541–604; trans. H. H. Gerth and Don Martindale as Ancient Judaism (Glencoe, Ill.: The Free Press, 1952): Gésammelte politische Schriften (Munich: Drei Masken Verlag, 1921); Politik als Beruf (Munich: Duncker & Humblot, 1919); Wissenschaft als Beruf (Munich: Duncker & Humblot, 1919); trans. Gerth and Mills in their earlier cited work as "Politics as a Vocation," and "Science as a Vocation," pp. 77–128 and 129–56, respectively.

4. Georg Simmel (1858–1918), philosopher and professor at Berlin and Strasbourg; Ernst Troeltsch (1865–1923), philosopher and professor at Bonn, Heidelberg, and Berlin.

5. Wilhelm Windelband (1848–1915), philosopher and

professor at Zürich, Freiburg, Strasbourg, and Heidelberg.
6. Weber became ill in 1898. From then on he suffered from periodic depressions.
7. Heinrich Rickert, Jr. (1863–1936), philosopher and professor at Freiburg and Heidelberg; Emil Kraepelin (1856–1926), psychiatrist and professor at Heidelberg and Munich.
8. See his article series, "Parlament und Regierung im neugeordneten Deutschland," *Frankfurter Zeitung*, summer 1917; parts of it trans. by Guenther Ross and Claus Wittich as "Parliament and Government in a Reconstructed Germany," in their edited work, *Economics and Society: An Outline of Interpretive Sociology* (Berkeley: University of California Press, 1977), Vol. 3, pp. 1381–1469.
9. In March 1916 Weber co-authored with Felix Somary "Der verschärfte U-Boot-Krieg," and distributed it to many party leaders, well-known parliamentarians, and the Foreign Ministry. For a text of it, see Johannes Winckelmann, ed., *Gesammelte politische Schriften*, 3d ed.; (Tübingen: J. C. B. Mohr (Paul Siebeck), 1971), pp. 146–54.
10. Johann Gottlieb Fichte (1762–1814), philosopher and the first major representative of transcendental idealism.

Max Weber: Politician, Scientist, Philosopher (1932)

1. A conversation which Jaspers heard in June 1914 between Max Weber and the constitutional law professor Fritz Fleiner (1867–1937) at Zürich, Basel, Tübingen, Heidelberg, and since 1915 again at Zürich. See his *Freiheit und Wiedervereinigung. Über Aufgaben deutscher Politik* (Munich: R. Piper & Co. Verlag, 1960), p. 41.

Notes

2. Lujo Brentano (1844–1931), economist and professor at Breslau, Strasbourg, Vienna, Leipzig, and Munich.
3. Quoted in Marianne Weber, *Max Weber. Ein Lebensbild* (Tübingen: J. C. B. Mohr (Paul Siebeck), 1926), p. 126.
4. Letter of 8 November 1884 to Hermann Baumgarten, in Max Weber, *Jugendbriefe* (Tübingen: J. C. B. Mohr (Paul Siebeck), 1936), p. 143.
5. This was written in 1887. See Marianne Weber, p. 127.
6. Ibid., p. 128.
7. Letter of 18 April 1892 to Baumgarten, ibid., p. 131.
8. Ibid.
9. May 1895 at Freiburg, entitled "Der Nationalstaat und die Volkswirtschaftspolitik," in *Gesammelte politische Schriften* (Munich: Drei Masken Verlag, 1921), pp. 7–30.
10. Ibid., p. 27.
11. Ibid., p. 28.
12. Ibid., p. 29.
13. Ibid.
14. Ibid.
15. Noteworthy are the *Frankfurter Zeitung* articles, "Deutschlands künftige Staatsform," November 1918, and "Das neue Deutschland," December 1918, reprinted in *Gesammelte politische Schriften* (1921), pp. 341–76 and 377–80, respectively.
16. Letter of 14 December 1906 to Friedrich Naumann, ibid., p. 451.
17. Letter of 10 February 1917 to Karl Löwenstein, ibid., pp. 467–68.
18. Erich Friedrich Wilhelm Ludendorff, quartermaster general in 1914, who in 1916 became Field Marshal Paul von Hindenburg's chief of staff (first quartermaster general) until the end of the war. Probably meant is Ludendorff's 21 March 1918 Western offensive, known as the Battle of Saint-Quentin.

19. Letter of 24 November 1918 to Friedrich Otto Crusius, in *Gesammelte politische Schriften* (1921), p. 482.
20. Letter of 18 November 1918 to Helene Weber, ibid.
21. Letter of 24 November 1918 to Crusius, ibid., p. 484.
22. Ibid.
23. Ibid.
24. Letter of 26 December 1918 to Crusius, ibid., p. 485.
25. Speech on 22 October 1916 in Munich, entitled "Deutschland unter den europäischen Weltmächten," ibid., p. 92.
26. Ibid., pp. 92–93.
27. Letter of 24 November 1918 to Crusius, ibid., pp. 483–84.
28. "Der Nationalstaat und die Volkswirtschaftspolitik," ibid., p. 30.
29. See Note 9 of the 1920 essay.
30. "Waffenstillstand und Frieden," *Frankfurter Zeitung*, 27 October 1918, in *Gesammelte politische Schriften* (1921), p. 340.
31. Letter of 11 October 1918 to Gerhart von Schulze-Gävernitz, ibid., p. 477.
32. Letter of 17 October 1918 to Naumann, ibid., p. 478.
33. Letter of 18 October 1918 to Naumann, ibid., p. 480.
34. The meeting took place in Berlin in June 1919 after Weber had returned from Versailles as a member of the German delegation. The following exchange took place: Ludendorff: "What is your idea of democracy, *then?*" Weber: "In a democracy the people elect a leader whom they trust. Then the elected says, 'Now shut your mouths and obey. The people and the parties are no longer permitted to contradict him.'" Ludendorff: "Such a 'democracy' could appeal to me!" Weber: "Afterwards the people can judge. If the leader has made mistakes—to the gallows with him! . . ." See Marianne Weber, p. 665.

Notes

35. Letter of 18 November 1918 to Helene Weber, in *Gesammelte politische Schriften* (1921), p. 481.
36. In Heidelberg on 2 January 1919, but to the German Democratic Party.
37. The colors of certain German student societies.
38. Letter, middle of April 1920 to Klara Mommsen, in Marianne Weber, p. 702.
39. "Politik als Beruf," in *Gesammelte politische Schriften* (1921), p. 447.
40. Ibid., p. 446.
41. Ibid.
42. Ibid.
43. Ibid., p. 448.
44. Ibid.
45. Ibid.
46. Ibid., p. 415.
47. Ibid., p. 434.
48. Ibid., p. 438.
49. Footnote to "Der verschärfte U-Boot-Krieg," ibid., p. 64.
50. Speech on 19 January 1920. Kurt Eisner (1867–1919), the Bavarian minister president, was shot on 21 February 1919. He had organized a socialist revolution on the night of 7 November 1918 that overthrew the Bavarian monarchy and proclaimed the Free State of Bavaria. Anton Graf von Arco-Valley (1897–1947), an Austrian, was sentenced to death on 16 January 1920, but the sentence was commuted to life imprisonment. In 1924 he was released from prison because of poor health.
51. Quoted in Marianne Weber, p. 673.
52. "Politik als Beruf," p. 436.
53. Written on 19 January 1920. Quoted in Marianne Weber, p. 685.
54. Marcus Ulpuis Nerva Trajan (53?–117 A.D.), Roman general and emperor.

55. Leopold von Ranke (1795–1886), leading German historian.

56. Gustav von Schmoller (1838–1917), economist and professor at Halle, Strasbourg, and Berlin.

57. Jacob Burckhardt (1818–1897), Swiss art historian and professor at Bonn, Basel, Berlin, and Zürich.

58. "Die 'Objektivität' sozialwissenschaftlicher und sozialpolitischer Erkenntnis," in *Gesammelte Aufsätze zur Wissenschaftslehre* (Tübingen: J. C. B. Mohr (Paul Siebeck), 1922), p. 184.

59. *Wirtschaft und Gesellschaft* (Tübingen: J. C. B. Mohr (Paul Siebeck), 1921), p. 13, Footnote 2.

60. "Die 'Objektivität' sozialwissenschaftlicher und sozialpolitischer Erkenntnis," p. 184.

61. "Wissenschaft als Beruf," in *Gesammelte Aufsätze zur Wissenschaftslehre*, p. 537.

62. Ibid., p. 550.

63. Ibid., p. 546.

64. Ibid., p. 550.

65. "Die Wirtschaftsethik der Weltreligionen," in *Gesammelte Aufsätze zur Religionssoziologie* (Tübingen: J. C. B. Mohr (Paul Siebeck), 1920), Vol. I, p. 537.

66. Letter of 17 January 1918, to Erich Trummler, in *Gesammelte politische Schriften* (1921), p. 474.

67. Introduction to "Die protestantische Ethik und der 'Geist' des Kapitalismus," in *Gesammelte Aufsätze zur Religionssoziologie*, p. 14.

68. "Wissenschaft als Beruf," p. 554.

69. Anicius Manlius Severinus Boethius (480–524), Roman philosopher, theologian, and statesman.

70. The case involved Adolf Koch (1855–?), professor of history and journalism at Heidelberg until his dismissal in 1913. The trial took place in 1910.

Notes

71. "Wissenschaft als Beruf," p. 555.
72. *Gesammelte Aufsätze zur Religionssoziologie*, Vol. III, p. V.
73. Quoted in Marianne Weber, p. 711.
74. Heinrich von Treitschke (1834–96), pro-Prussian and Hohenzollern historian and professor at Leipzig, Freiburg, Kiel, and Berlin, also *Reichstag* member from 1871 until 1884.
75. Letter to Baumgarten, 25 April 1887, in *Jugendbriefe*, p. 233.
76. Count de Mirabeau (1749–91), French orator and revolutionary leader.

Max Weber: Concluding Characterization (1960–1961)

1. These are notes for his 1960–61 lectures. The words in brackets are Hans Saner's additions. The original had dashes at the end of some of the sentences. They have been deleted. Since these are lecture notes, some of the sentences are incomplete. Some interpolations have been made, in the interests of clarity.
2. *Max Weber. Eine Gedenkrede* (Tübingen: J. C. B. Mohr (Paul Siebeck), 1921).
3. *Max Weber. Deutsches Wesen im politischen Denken, im Forschen und Philosophieren* (Oldenburg: Gerhard Stalling, 1932).
4. *Gesammelte Aufsätze zur Religionssoziologie* (Tübingen: J. C. B. Mohr (Paul Siebeck), 1921), Vol. III, p. V.
5. See Note 9 of the 1932 essay.

6. From then on he suffered from periodic depressions.
7. Friedrich Naumann (1860–1919), politician and a co-founder of the German Democratic Party in November 1918.
8. See Note 7 of the 1920 essay.
9. Quoted in Marianne Weber, *Max Weber. Ein Lebensbild* (Tübingen: J. C. B. Mohr (Paul Siebeck), 1926), p. 711.
10. Friedrich Hölderlin (1770–1843), poet.
11. See Note 4 of the 1920 essay.
12. This section was mostly written in 1924.
13. From here on, a later text.
14. Meant here is Theodor Heuss (1884–1963), the first president, 1949–59.
15. Here again it is the 1924 text.

Observations on Max Weber's Political Thought (1962)

1. See Note 9 of the 1932 essay.
2. "Der Nationalstaat und die Volkswirtschaftspolitik," in *Gesammelte politische Schriften* (Munich: Drei Masken Verlag, 1921), p. 27.
3. Speech in Mannheim on 13 December 1897, quoted in Wolfgang Mommsen, *Max Weber und die deutsche Politik 1890–1920,* 2nd ed. (Tübingen: J. C. B. Mohr (Paul Siebeck), 1974), p. 82.
4. Ibid., pp. 82–83.
5. "Der Nationalstaat und die Volkswirtschaftspolitik," p. 30.
6. Ibid., p. 29.
7. Ibid., p. 30.
8. Ibid.

Notes

9. Letter of 10 February 1917 to Karl Löwenstein, in *Gesammelte politische Schriften* (1921), pp. 467–68.
10. Letter of 24 November 1918 to Friedrich Otto Crusius, ibid., p. 483.
11. Ibid.
12. Ibid.
13. Ibid., p. 484.
14. Letter of 26 December 1918 to Crusius, ibid., p. 485.
15. Letter of 24 November 1918 to Crusius, ibid., p. 484.
16. Letter of 26 December 1918 to Crusius, ibid., p. 485.
17. Quoted in Mommsen, p. 45, Footnote 32.
18. "Wahlrecht und Demokratie," December 1917, in *Gesammelte politische Schriften* (1921), p. 312.
19. A Hessian town, fifty kilometres south of Kassel.
20. Letter of 12 November 1908 to Friedrich Naumann, in ibid., p. 457.
21. Adolf von Harnack (1851–1930), Protestant theologian and professor at Leipzig, Gießen, Marburg, and Berlin.
22. Letter of 5 February 1906 to Harnack, in Mommsen, p. 181.
23. Quoted in ibid., p. 100.
24. See Note 14 of the 1932 essay.
25. Letter of 24 November 1918 to Crusius, in *Gesammelte politische Schriften* (1921), pp. 483–84.
26. Josef Alois Schumpeter (1883–1950), Austrian economist and professor at Czernowitz, Graz, Bonn, and Harvard.
27. Felix Somary (1881–1956), Austrian economist. The quotations about the conversation are from his book, *Erinnerungen aus meinem Leben* (Zürich: Manesse Verlag, 1959), pp. 171–72.
28. Ludo Moritz Hartmann (1865–1924), Austrian historian and politician.
29. The conversation took place in the *Café-Restaurant Landt-*

mann in the Ringstraße, now Dr. Karl Lueger-Ring, during the 1918 summer term at the University of Vienna.

30. Martin Luther's (1483–1546) statement before the Diet of Worms on 18 April 1521.

31. "Politik als Beruf," in *Gesammelte politische Schriften* (1921), pp. 448–49.

32. Ibid., p. 450.

33. "Der Sinn der 'Wertfreiheit' der soziologischen und ökonomischen Wissenschaften," in *Gesammelte Aufsätze zur Wissenschaftslehre* (Tübingen: J. C. B. Mohr (Paul Siebeck), 1922), p. 502.

34. Bernhard Knipperdolling (?–1536), Anabaptist mayor of Münster.

35. Quoted in Marianne Weber, *Max Weber. Ein Lebensbild* (Tübingen: J. C. B. Mohr (Paul Siebeck), 1926), p. 711.

Letters to Hannah Arendt (1966)

1. Hannah Arendt (1906–75), student of Jaspers, philosopher and professor at Chicago and the New School for Social Research.

2. Ricarda Huch (1864–1947), writer.

3. Wolfgang J. Mommsen, *Max Weber und die deutsche Politik 1890–1920* (Tübingen: J. C. B. Mohr (Paul Siebeck), 1959), 2nd ed., 1974); trans. Michael S. Steinberg as *Max Weber and German Politics, Eighteen Ninety to Nineteen Twenty* (Chicago and London: The University of Chicago Press, 1985).

4. Quoted in Marianne Weber, *Max Weber. Ein Lebensbild* (Tübingen: J. C. B. Mohr (Paul Siebeck), 1926), p. 711.

5. Alfred Weber (1868–1958), brother of Max Weber, economist and professor at Prague and Heidelberg.

Notes

6. (Berlin: J. Springer, 1919).
7. Stefan George (1868–1933), lyric poet.
8. Richard Thoma (1874–1957), constitutional lawyer and professor at Heidelberg.
9. One of the main Heidelberg streets along the Neckar River.
10. Hermann Oncken (1869–1945), historian and professor at Chicago, Gießen, Heidelberg, Munich, and Berlin.
11. Eduard Spranger (1882–1963), philosopher and psychologist and professor at Leipzig, Berlin, and Tübingen.
12. *Geschichte des Vereins für Sozialpolitik, 1872–1932. Im Auftrage des Liquidationsausschusses verfaßt vom Schriftführer Dr. Franz Boese* (Berlin: Duncker & Humblot, 1939), Franz Boese, ed.

Index of Names

INDEX

Index

von Richthofen, Else, *see*
    Jaffé, Else

Weber, Alfred, 187
Weber, Marianne, *xiv–xv*,
    122
Weber, Max
    birth of, 56
    Commemorative Address
      on (1920), 3–27
    death of, *xvi*, 36, 67, 170,
      186
    friendship with Jaspers,
      xiv–xvi
    as human being, 110–24
    Jaspers' letters to Hannah
      Arendt about,
      185–91
    love affair of, *xix–x*
    as philosopher, 34, 37–38,
      103–35, 140, 142–43,
      155, 157
    as politician and political
      thinker, 31–32,
      36–37, 39–73,
      146–51, 157, 163–82
    as scientist, 32–33, 36,
      74–102, 144–46, 157,
      188–89
    skeptics and opponents of,
      153–54
    as universal historian,
      82–85, 86–87
    at Versailles, *xviii*, 51
Wilhelm II, *xxii*, 47, 50,
    58–59, 64, 147, 149,
    169, 180
Wilson, Woodrow, 57–58,
    175
Windelband, Wilhelm, 13

211

Index of Subjects

INDEX

Index

INDEX